Praise for *The Think Tank Racket*

"A necessary and vital analysis of the corrupt and corrupting influence of think tanks on policy and the policy process. Diesen shows how they are part of the echo chamber funded by defense contractors and associated ministries and corporations in the service of an ill-advised militarism, especially in regard to Russia, which has created a situation of permanent global war. The work throws a shaft of light on a dark corner of contemporary world politics, and exposes the dangers of unelected 'thinkers' on elected practitioners. Essential reading for anyone concerned with the future of democracy."

PROFESSOR RICHARD SAKWA, University of Kent

"In this excellent book, Professor Diesen explores the intrusive and growing political influence of think tanks. U.S. foreign policy is further militarized as think tanks pursue a business model of selling political influence to the military-industrial complex."

CLARE DALY, Member of European Parliament

"German Bundestag Member Sevim Dagdelen, referring to media coverage of Ukraine, has warned, *'Es ist unsere erste Pflicht, sich von diesem Koenigreich der Luegen nicht dumm machen zu lassen'*—'Our first duty is not to let ourselves be made dumb by this kingdom of lies.' And so, dutifully, and with truth as his breastplate, Glenn Diesen gives us the wherewithal to see that kingdom for what it is, and to expose its hirelings—the Knights of the Think Tanks."

RAY McGOVERN, former CIA officer and chair of National Intelligence Estimates

"Glenn Diesen provides an important but disturbing account of the nexus between think tanks, governments, and the military-industrial complex. Instead of producing well-informed analyses, think tanks promote the interests of those who fund them, while seeking to suppress any manifestations of dissent. *The Think Tank Racket* is a troubling but necessary read for all those wanting a better-informed political landscape."

PROFESSOR PAUL ROBINSON, University of Ottawa

THE THINK TANK RACKET

Managing the Information War Against Russia

GLENN DIESEN

Clarity Press, Inc.

ISBN: 978-1-949762-80-8
EBOOK ISBN: 978-1-949762-81-5

In-house editor: Diana G. Collier
Book design: Becky Luening

Library of Congress Control Number: 2023940300

Clarity Press, Inc.
2625 Piedmont Rd. NE, Ste. 56
Atlanta, GA 30324, USA
https://www.claritypress.com

Table of Contents

1. Introducing the Think Tank Industry

In swanky conference rooms, with bottles of fancy water brands scattered across tables, the West's policymaking elites gather to sing from their hymn sheets. There is little, if any, disagreement because they have come to confirm their own biases rather than conduct real debates. When evening arrives, they retire to expensive restaurants where they slap each other on the back and grandiosely refer to themselves as "Atlanticists" or "Fellows." Here, opposing nations and different points of view have no agency of their own; they are only useful to the extent that they contribute to a pre-ordained narrative.

These are the people who run the think tank movement. And their job is to manufacture consent for the goals of their paymasters—who, these days, are overwhelmingly drawn from the arms industry, and other vested interests that benefit from tensions with Russia and certain other states. The community is tightly knit and well paid. It enjoys huge power due to its ability to influence politics and manipulate the mainstream media. However, the general public is generally unaware of this phenomenon. The public has no idea that the seemingly benign experts who write policy papers and turn up in the media to offer authoritative views are often beholden to the think tank trough. Media consumers are rarely if ever, warned about how the views and opinions of these pundits are not neutral or objective, but are in actuality sponsored opinions, providing a gloss of objectivity while promoting their sponsors' interests.

In theory, and as reflected in public perception, think tanks are supposed to be unbiased and objective research institutions that connect academia with decision-makers to deliver the most informed and optimal foreign policy. The reality is that the think tank business model instead tends to undermine the principle of academic inquiry and to corrupt political decision-making. As this book will demonstrate, rather than asking questions and seeking answers through intellectual pluralism to pursue the best foreign policy, the think tanks stifle intellectual diversity of thought as they are in the business of policy advocacy on behalf of their donors. Indeed, the funders of think tanks are not paying for contributions in the media to create an informed public; rather their incentive derives from instrumentalizing this optimal means of public indoctrination and manufacturing of consent.

The Rise and Corruption of the Expert Class

Politicians are expected to make decisions on a wide variety of complex topics on which they often have limited expertise. As the world becomes increasingly complex, it is simply unrealistic to expect elected leaders to have sufficient expertise in all areas of policy-making. Politicians are supposed to have an in-depth understanding of topics ranging from immigration reforms, fiscal policies, crime prevention, Russian industrial policy, Chinese weapons manufacturing, naval strategies, digitalization, ethnic tensions in Ethiopia, social stability in India, political polarization in Brazil, European integration, and language laws in Kazakhstan. Clearly, this is a mission impossible.

Politicians are therefore reliant on partnerships with academics to provide the required expertise. This can be a challenging partnership as a common language is often absent. Academics pursue a scientific approach to developing knowledge, which implies that much of their research focuses on theory and method to make sense of how the world works and why states behave the way they do. However, what political decision-makers need to navigate through an increasingly convoluted world are clear policy papers with analyses that provide policy recommendations in response to specific challenges.

Think tanks responded to this demand and emerged with the explicit purpose of providing politicians with expert insights and analyses to specifically assist policy-making, thus functioning as a bridge between academia and political decision-making. The think tanks also serve as a source of reliable (and non-controversial) information and expert opinion for the media. As a result, they have an immense influence over the development of narratives, policies, and laws. But who are the experts and who are they accountable to? Who funds this expert class?

Think tanks are mostly funded by powerful lobbying groups, ranging from the military-industrial complex to foreign governments and interests. These investors buy the source credibility of "independent experts" that can marginalize academics and journalists to infiltrate and shape public opinion and policy. Insofar as they are reliant on their funders, think tanks have become a symptom of hyper-capitalism in which all aspects of society have become an appendage to the market. Even political influence is regulated by the free market, in which think tanks are an important component.

If one can control the source of information that decision-makers act upon—does it matter who is democratically elected into office? It is well-known that the concentration of power undermines democracy. Alexis de Tocqueville famously argued in the early 19th century that the democratic spirit in America was stronger than in France as there was less concentration of wealth in America, and American civil servants were paid much less (Piketty 2014: 188, 527). Almost two centuries later, the U.S. has accrued an immense amount of capital that is increasingly concentrated in the hands of a few elites. Inevitably, this corrupts the democratic spirit in America that Tocqueville once admired and considered the gold standard. When society is regulated and organized by the marketplace, it is hardly a conspiracy theory to recognize that the concentration of capital influences all aspects of society, including the development of knowledge. The power-knowledge nexus suggests that power is used to create new knowledge by influencing associations and meanings, making the control of knowledge and language a source of power (Foucault 2019). The control of knowledge is a more efficient and enduring insgtrument to enable exploitation or oppression, compared to blunt coercion. Those with power determine what knowledge is to be constructed that society will then interpret as reality, and in turn, their control over knowledge is a principal source of their power. Think tanks have ecome to provide an ideal case study of how corporate power can seize control over knowledge and thus over policy.

Matthew Rojansky, the director of the Wilson Center's think tank, the Kennan Institute, penned an article in which he reflected on why his industry is becoming increasingly corrupted. Rojansky argues that think tanks serve the positive function of creating policy professionals, while acknowledging their growing weakness is the business model they follow in which political influence and access are put up for sale. Many think tanks do not even bother to uphold the illusion of objective analysis as they "have become advocacy groups, or even lobbyists, by another name," simply as a function of market forces as "political parties want loyal propagandists, not niggling, equivocating academic hangers-on. And potential donors want veteran sharpshooters to fire their policy bullets into exactly the right target at precisely the right moment" (Rojansky and Shapiro 2021). Subsequently, the lack of transparency undermines the credibility of think tanks as honest brokers.

While universities are structured to pursue knowledge, they are simply not capable of competing against the wealthy and mighty think tanks for influence. In a *New York Times* article, Thomas Frank cautioned that real academics were pushed aside and replaced with cliché-spouting operatives that can position themselves as intellectual heavy weights as their industries had "grown into a powerful quasi-academy with seven-figure budgets and phalanxes of 'senior fellows' and 'distinguished chairs'" (Frank 2006).

The president of the American Enterprise Institute (AEI), Christopher DeMuth, explained how his think tank established its political influence: "We try to get in the newspaper op-ed pages and hawk our books and magazines much more aggressively than a university would feel comfortable with" (McCartney and McCartney 2015:

64). The media subsequently contact the media-savvy AEI frequently when they need "expert opinions," although almost always without revealing which special interests funds their multi-million-dollar operations of producing knowledge. Making matters worse, think tanks have also become the go-to source for the U.S. Congress.

Source Credibility: Constructing and Selling an Expert Class

Academia is a meritocracy in which the establishment and ranking of experts depend on the competition of ideas, in which the strongest theories and arguments rise to the top. In contrast, with think tanks it is the marketplace that dictates which ideas should rise to the top. The business model incentivizes think tanks to follow the money as the most powerful interests can buy their own expert class to dominate the media and politics. In such an environment, it is the ability to construct the illusion of objectivity and expertise that determines which arguments ascend to the top.

Think tanks recognize that source credibility is an indispensable component of effective communication. The concept of source credibility was developed in Aristotle's *The Rhetoric*, which outlined how persuasion depends on ethos—the character of the communicator that communicates competency and moral authority (McCroskey 1966). Credible communication therefore requires a source that is deemed to be trustworthy and an expert. Social experiments demonstrate that the persuasiveness of messaging changes profoundly by merely introducing a different communicator (Hovland and Weiss 1951).

Constructing source credibility is therefore considered to be a key component of propaganda (Diesen 2022). Without source credibility, the communication can even be counter-productive. Thus, the entire notion that state-owned media are the main purveyors of propaganda is fundamentally flawed as "historically, intelligence services and propaganda institutions have posed as ordinary citizens to assume a credibility that they lack in their own roles" (Golovchenko, Hartmann and Adler-Niessen 2018: 992).

Propaganda can be conceptualized as herding the masses, and a key element is thus the construction of authority figures and experts to herd the public towards the desired opinions. Walter Lippmann (1922) argued that the world is too complex for any individual to comprehend, which is why societies need people and institutions that can collect, analyze and disseminate information. Thus, the public looks towards an expert class to guide the masses: "In making up its mind its first impulse is usually to follow the example of a trusted leader [an icon or celebrity]. This is one of the most firmly established principles of mass psychology" (Bernays 1928: 50).

Think tanks' insertion in the media has the purpose of directing the public towards the "right" conclusions and opinions, as opposed to merely educating a population into making an educated and independent decision. A brilliant achievement of propaganda has been to convince the population that propaganda is only an instrument of authoritarian states and not liberal democracies. Walter Lippman, Edward Bernays, and other academics behind the initial literature on propaganda from the 1920s, argued that democracies are *more* inclined to embrace propaganda to manufacture consent.

When the public is the sovereign and the source of legitimate power, there is an even greater incentive to manipulate public opinion (Mills 1956). Democracy relies on propaganda to organize a shared identity and opinions, which is the foundation for social cohesion in an increasingly large and complex society (Merriam 1925; Lasswell 1927; Bernays 1928; Mead 1934). Along the way, the objective of directing the public in the right direction was replaced with directing the public in the direction of the highest bidder.

Open societies make propaganda seemingly more difficult, although it also enables propaganda to camouflage itself. During the Cold War, propaganda was portrayed as principally an instrument of authoritarian communist states. Convincing the audience that the West does not use propaganda is imperative for the effectiveness of the propaganda. In reality, scholars recognized that Western propaganda was more efficient than communist propaganda because it could be concealed by mobilizing private industry and organizations (Hixson 1998). In contrast, the obvious propaganda initiatives by the Soviets were more blatant and thus less efficient.

That the strategy of source credibility was deliberate was made explicit by George Kennan (1948: 4), who argued for covert operations through private intermediaries: "General direction and financial support would come from the Government; guidance and funds would pass to a private American organization or organizations (perhaps 'business' enterprises) composed of private citizens."

But who funds these organizations, who works for them, and what are the real agendas at play? From the start, let's be clear, the term "think tank" essentially amounts to a more polite way of saying "lobby group." They exist to serve—and promote—the agendas of their funders. However, particularly in the United States, the field has become increasingly shady and disingenuous, with lobbyists being given faux academic titles like "Senior Non-Resident Fellow" and "Junior Adjunct Fellow" to distinguish them from honest registered lobbyists. And this smokescreen usually serves to cloud the real goals of these operations.

How Think Tanks Influence Policies toward Russia

This book argues that exploring the role of think tanks is imperative to understanding U.S. policies toward Russia, and represents a first step in this heretofore unexplored territory. Throughout the entirety of history, there have been rulers and advisors seeking to influence these rulers. Think tanks are an industry of such influencers. The main income for these influencers is the weapons industry, which flourishes in times of conflict. Inventing or exacerbating threats then becomes a business. The demand for weapons during the Cold War could to some extent be replaced by the global war on terror, although there is no better-imagined enemy than Russia following decades of conflict. Recreating the Russian threat has made the conflict a self-fulfilling prophecy.

Think tanks have an immense influence on decision-making, yet this influence is largely unexplored. Much research and focus are devoted to the corrupting impact of powerful interest groups and lobbying groups which diminish the relevance of the voters and hollow out democracy. Yet, the think tanks have attracted much less significance despite their corrupting business model and their central role in influencing the political decision-makers, the media, and the public.

Think tanks also function as a waiting room for politicians before returning to government. In a revolving door system, politicians in high positions are integrated into think tanks when they are out of office, which allows them to remain active and still in the game until returning to power. The think tanks buy themselves credibility and influence by featuring their important and publicly recognized names and get to cultivate their positions before helping them return to government. The think tanks are then able to inform their donors that their own people are now roaming the halls of power. The think tanks make a living from conflicting interests; it is not a bug but a feature of the system. It is seemingly too late to address this corrupting impact on politics as the think tanks have already infected all parts of the system.

These pseudo-academic institutions function as lobbyists that sell political influence in myriad areas of policy. In the United Kingdom, they lend legitimacy to tobacco manufacturers, and over in Washington, they serve to whitewash the Gulf States with questionable human rights and foreign policy records. They are also used by states and private actors to impose agendas way beyond their frontiers. For instance, thinks tanks pushing a pro-American or pro-NATO agenda in Eastern Europe are almost all funded by various U.S. government agencies or cut-outs, such as the National Endowment for Democracy or the State Department in Washington itself.

The NGOs are important as they fund many of the think tanks, and in fact, there are remarkable parallels between the NGOs and think tanks. NGO is the acronym for "non-governmental organization," which is often a deceptive term as NGOs are funded almost completely by the governments and staffed by people with former positions in the intelligence services. Much like the think tanks, the NGOs accrue source credibility by pretending to be independent, by clothing themselves in the "non-governmental" terminology—despite often being funded by governments and staffed by former government officials and intelligence officers.

The think tanks took off during the Reagan years, and this is also the date of the founding of the National Endowment for Democracy (NED), the most noteworthy NGO in terms of funding and cooperating with think tanks. NED is renowned for its central role in fomenting color-revolutions across the post-Soviet space. In the West, the color revolutions are referred to as organic democratic revolutions, while in Russia they are denounced as Western-backed coups.

NED was established in 1983 as a private organization, even though it was inaugurated by President Ronald Reagan and funded by the U.S. Congress. The NGO formula was to "hide in plain sight" by reducing reliance on covert operations that could be exposed and cause embarrassment, and instead make coups overt under the legitimacy of promoting democracy and freedom. Simply put, U.S. subversion of adversarial states is to be viewed as legitimate as long as all competing national interests and conflicts are framed as a rivalry between democracy and authoritarianism, or freedom and slavery. Think tanks similarly make conflicting interests and corporate lobbying respectable under the veil of being research institutions.

Reagan asserted at the inauguration ceremony of NED: "This program will not be hidden in shadows. It'll stand proudly in the spotlight, and that's where it belongs. We can and should be proud of our message of democracy." Allen Weinstein, a cofounder of NED, acknowledged that "a lot of what we do today was done covertly 25 years ago by the CIA" (Ignatius 1991). By the late 1980s, NED began providing funding to anti-communist groups and subversive activities within the Soviet bloc. *Washington Post* reporter David Ignatius (1991) penned an article with the title "The new world of spyless coups," in which he argued that NED has been the "sugar daddy of overt operations." This enabled Washington to support regime change under the auspices of "democracy promotion," paramilitary operations under the guise of backing "freedom fighters," and what used to be called "propaganda" can now simply be referred to as "information."

Philip Agee, a CIA whistle-blower, explained that NED was established as a "propaganda and inducement program" to subvert foreign nations and legitimize the subversion by styling it as a democracy promotion initiative (Stevenson 2021: 241). CIA Director William J. Casey wrote a letter to Edwin Meese, a White House counselor to President Reagan, advocating for the establishment of a "National Endowment," although recognizing the CIA needed to maintain a distance: "Obviously we here [at the CIA] should not get out front in the development of such an organization, nor do we wish to appear to be a sponsor or advocate" (Parry 2015a). The *Guardian* described the 2004 Orange Revolution in Ukraine as "an American creation, a sophisticated and brilliantly conceived exercise in western branding and mass marketing," which replicated the template of "winning other people's elections" as had been done in Serbia and Georgia (Traynor 2004). Another article by the *Guardian* referred to the Orange Revolution as a "postmodern coup d'état" and a "CIA-sponsored third world uprising of cold war days, adapted to post-Soviet conditions" (Steele 2004).

The disarming label "NGO" enables ever-more direct intrusion into the domestic affairs of other states such as Russia. Case in point: Navalny's NGO, the Anti-Corruption Foundation (ACF), has long been suspected of working for British intelligence services. British diplomat James Ford, whom the FSB asserts is an MI6 intelligence agent, was caught on tape with Vladimir Ashurkov, Navalny's right-hand man and Executive Director at the ACF, requesting $10–$20 million from Ford to finance Navalny's campaign. He also asked for any compromising material that the British may have on Russian officials. While Ashurkov's attempt to collude with a foreign government was captured, Ford did not make any offers on the tape. However, by 2022, there was no longer any pretense of the ACF not colluding with British intelligence. The Navalny NGO itself announced that: "The Anti-Corruption Foundation, at the request of the UK, has prepared an abbreviated list of the main warmongers who should be sanctioned first." One can only imagine the reactions from London if the roles were reversed and a British NGO was boasting that they were working on behalf of the Russian foreign ministry. "Hybrid-warfare" would then be considered too soft of an accusation.

In recent years, think tanks have especially been at the forefront of the information war against Russia, which is mainly pushed by the

U.S. and its British allies. The U.S.-backed outfits are usually very clever in how they package their work. It's typically presented as "democracy promotion" or support for "civil society," using this as an ideological cover for pushing local elites to integrate into American-led institutions like NATO. Some may feel a more suitable term would be modern "empire building."

The purpose of academia is the creation of new knowledge, developing scientific methods to pursue objective truths to inform the public and policymakers, whereas think tanks today offer tailored policies for sale. As the veteran Moscow correspondent John Helmer (2015) notes:

> [T]ere are about 450 think-tanks in Europe and the U.S. currently focusing on international relations, war, peace, and economic security. Of these, about one hundred regularly analyze Russian affairs. And of these, less than ten are not committed antagonists of Russia. That is barely two percent of the intellectual materiel which can be counted as non-partisan or neutral in the information war now underway between the NATO alliance and Russia. In this balance of forces, think-tanks behave like tanks—that's the weapon, not the cistern.

There is no need to pay think tankers to take a position they do not believe in; rather the think tanks merely hire the experts who have reached the "correct" conclusion. This practice is often extended to the media as well. Those who believe the international system consists of states with competing interests and that peace requires mutual understanding and compromise will have a hard time finding employment. In contrast, great careers await those who believe the world is a struggle between good and evil, and permanent peace can only be reached when the virtuous in Washington defeat the wicked. Case in point: a *New York Times* job posting for the role as a foreign correspondent in Russia presented the following job posting:

> Vladimir Putin's Russia remains one of the biggest stories in the world. It sends out hit squads armed with nerve agents against its enemies, most recently the opposition leader Aleksei Navalny. It has its cyber agents sow chaos and disharmony in the West to tarnish its democratic systems, while promoting its faux version of democracy. It has deployed private military contractors around the globe to secretly spread its influence. At home, its hospitals are filling up fast with Covid patients as its president hides out in his villa. If that sounds like a place you want to cover, then we have good news: We will have an opening for a new correspondent as Andy Higgins takes over as our next Eastern Europe Bureau Chief early next year. (Robinson 2020).

Needless to say, there is no reason to apply if you are of the opinion that the deterioration of U.S.-Russian relations is caused by the absence of a pan-European security architecture. However, if the solution to deteriorating relations is more weapons and getting tougher on Russia, then *The New York Times* and the think tanks in Washington may have a job for you.

Promoters of Conflict

A remarkable feature of think tanks is that they almost always advise western leaders to adopt an aggressive posture toward Moscow or other external capitals the West likely finds disagreeable. However, few, if any, ever suggest ways to improve or even normalize relations. Surely the purpose of a policy advisory should be to outline various scenarios from across a wide spectrum of possibilities that politicians and officials could draw from when formulating plans? After all, even ordinary folk should have a contingency plan or two just in case their circumstances change.

Yet, on the Russia beat, it is just one-way traffic, with the kind of narratives to be found in a Marvel Comic or Harry Potter: goodies and baddies. Naturally, the Russians always assumed the latter role, as the foil to Captain America. The same focus applies to any other state which displeases Washington and London's movers and shakers. Every leader of an adversarial country becomes the new Hitler, and the only history book on the shelf for reference is on Munich 1938 to remind everyone that, in a struggle against evil, compromise is appeasement.

In a world where U.S. policies are under the heavy influence of think tanks, the policies towards Russia will unavoidably produce confrontation. When peace is bad for business and conflict fills the coffers, then cooperation is tantamount to appeasement and confrontation is virtuous.

2. The Rise of the Think Tank Industry

The modern think tank industry has been developing for more than 100 years, creating a new expert class and connecting them with elected officials. Think tanks in the U.S. originally entered the marketplace of ideas with benign intentions. Civic leaders and reformers from the political Left and political Right aimed to address the socioeconomic challenges as society industrialized and became increasingly complex. Think tanks were thus seen as an instrument to create a more professional government. They were intended to function as nonpartisan and independent factories of new ideas. Yet, success can be a curse. Once these think tanks became more influential, their subsequent power began to corrupt their initial function.

Over the years, Washington's policies have become very dependent on the think tanks. In fact, the relationship between think tanks, the government, and the media has become increasingly blurred over the years. Think tanks hire former government officials and the relationship continues as they move back into government, while also offering "expert reports" and interviews to journalists. With democratic governance and journalism outsourced to the marketplace, what could go wrong? An unfortunate consequence of the rise of think tanks is the willingness to abandon inquiry in favor of conformity to the zeitgeist they help to create.

The Origin of Think Tanks

The modern think tank emerged from the process of seeking counsel that can be said to originate in the Europe of the Dark Ages. That's 9th-century France, to be precise. Their roots lie in the way medieval popes and monarchs were advised at court about everything from taxation to foreign policy. For instance, back in the days of Henry VIII, the English king may have asked a few experts to give him some projections on the effects of splitting from Rome. Or the Holy Roman Emperor Charlemagne might have taken counsel on how things might play out under his plan to reunite most of Western Europe for the first time in hundreds of years.

The process became a bit more formal by the 19th century, when outfits like the Royal United Services Institute for Defence and Security Studies (previously the Royal United Services Institution) or RUSI, for short, were founded. RUSI started in 1831, with the backing of the Irish statesman and soldier Arthur Wellesley, better known as the Duke of Wellington. RUSI exists to this day.

The rise of socialism was also aided by a think tank, in this case, the Fabian Society, from which the British Labour Party later sprouted, 16 years after its 1884 birth. The Fabians quickly attracted quite a line-up, including famous names, such as H.W. Wells, George Bernard Shaw, Emmeline Pankhurst, and Ramsay MacDonald, among its early members.

The size and responsibilities of government increased as industrial society became increasingly complex. The subsequent gap in expertise demanded that elected officials form closer ties with an expert class to address the new responsibilities. The Carnegie Endowment for International Peace was established in 1910 and became the first think tank devoted exclusively to foreign policy. The Institute for Government Research, which later became the Brookings Institution, prepared the U.S. economy for the First World War.

The utilization of think tanks went global as the First World War concluded in 1919, although you could argue America had already had a taste of something similar from its colonial-era pamphleteers. British and American delegates to the Versailles peace conference held a dinner at Paris's Hotel Majestic where the idea of an Anglo-American institute to connect the declining British Empire with the new superpower, the U.S., was first conceived. The idea was stillborn, although a few decades later, a number of similar trans-Atlantic initiatives would come to fruition.

Colonel Edward House, an advisor of President Woodrow Wilson, brought together leading scholars to study the various options for a post-war foreign policy. This group, consisting of New York bankers, lawyers, and academics, formed the Council on Foreign Relations (CFR) in 1921. The Royal Institute for International Affairs (known as Chatham House) had been created some months earlier in London. As *The Economist* notes, "they have served as templates for numerous other think-tanks around the world" (Economist 2019).

Think Tanks during the Cold War

After the Second World War, a new wave of think tanks emerged. The RAND Corporation was established in 1948 by Douglas Aircraft Company to connect military planning with scientific research and development. RAND Corporation has remained closely linked with U.S. intelligence services ever since and cooperates with multiple universities. Similar think tanks devoted to influencing Cold War policies emerged.

The evolution of the think tank industry continued. Advocacy think tanks with lobbying functions emerged in the 1960s. In the 1970s and 1980s, yet another wave of think tanks developed that were more policy specific and partisan. As this new center of power accrued more political power and influence, think tanks unavoidably became competitors for informing policymakers and the media. The Heritage Foundation was founded in 1973 as an explicitly conservative think tank with close ties cultivated with the Republican Party. Similarly, the CATO Institute was established in 1977 to advance libertarian ideas. These conservative think tanks were to a large extent a response to the liberal think tanks.

Many American conservatives believed a liberal agenda had begun to undermine their conservative principles during the 1960s and 1970s. Accordingly, conservatives developed think tanks such as the American Enterprise Institute and the Heritage Foundation to push for key ideas such as reducing the size of the federal government, decreasing taxes, cutting welfare, and restoring U.S. economic strength. Simply put, the think tanks were created to pursue research to support pre-established ideological objectives. President Reagan's policies were profoundly influenced by the policy recommendations of the Heritage Foundation; that such entities could be a source of power was not missed. Subsequently, the think tank industry grew rapidly from the 1980s and played an increasingly larger role in shaping U.S. policies. The think tanks have naturally positioned themselves as leaning either to the political Left or Right, becoming political echo chambers organized according to the ideological rivalry of the Democrat and Republican parties.

Think Tanks after the Cold War

The think tank business experienced a great boom in the era of globalization, as their influence continued to grow, and they increasingly became transnational. Foreign states, organizations, and individuals subsequently recognized that sponsoring think tanks was necessary in order to curry favor in Washington. Research by the Transparency Initiative at the Center for International Policy revealed that between 2014 and 2018, foreign governments gave $175 million to the top 50 think tanks in the U.S. (Freeman 2020a). As many politicians are offered a paid position in think tanks, the elected officials have other and more direct loyalties than merely their voters.

The New York Times acknowledges that think tanks obtain their influence by faking independence: "think tanks, which position themselves as 'universities without students,' have power in government policy debates because they are seen as researchers independent of moneyed interests." However, "in the chase for funds, think tanks are pushing agendas important to corporate donors, at times blurring the line between researchers and lobbyists. And they are doing so while reaping the benefits of their tax-exempt status, sometimes without disclosing their connections to corporate interests" (Lipton and Williams

2016). If the think tanks were truly independent and could legitimately argue that their funding does not impact their findings, then they should not fear disclosing where their money comes from.

These days, there is often little difference between a think tank and a lobbying firm. Except, as a rule, think tankers are not subject to the same regulations as straight-up influence peddlers. Back in 2014, *The New York Times* ran a report on how "Foreign Powers Buy Influence at Think Tanks" (Lipton and Williams 2014). It hinged on how Norway had plowed $5 million into the Center for Global Development, which is mainly focused on policy in the developing world. On the surface, Norway's intentions seemed benign. Oslo wanted to push the U.S. government to double its spending on a foreign aid program—specifically, slowing the clearing of forests in Indonesia. But it served to expose how opaque the line had become between lobbying and think tanking. More digging showed how this can work: "American research groups, after receiving money from Norway, have advocated in Washington for enhancing Norway's role in NATO, promoted its plans to expand oil drilling in the Arctic, and pushed its climate change agenda" (Lipton and Williams 2014).

As the lawyer Joseph Sandler told the *Times*' reporters "think tanks have this patina of academic neutrality and objectivity, and that is being comprised" (Lipton and Williams 2014). However, the real meat was towards the article's end. It revealed how the agreement which secured Norway's largesse imposed very specific demands on the Center for Global Development. The research organization, in return for the cash, was not simply asked to publish reports on combating climate change. It was also obliged to "persuade Washington officials to double United States spending on global forest protection efforts to $500 million a year" (Lipton and Williams 2014). Given Norway is a huge Carbon producer (with an economy reliant on oil), its motives may not have been only altruistic.

The *NYT* article also cited the Brookings Institution, the Center for Strategic and International Studies, and the Atlantic Council, pointing out how "each is a major recipient of overseas funds, producing policy papers, hosting forums and organizing private briefings for senior United States government officials that typically align with the foreign governments' agendas" (Lipton and Williams 2014).

The Norwegian Centre for Conflict Resolution published a paper that recognized the pervasive influence of think tanks in the U.S.:

> Think thanks play an important role both in providing research and recommendations to the U.S. administration and by supplying staff to key government positions. The revolving door between think tanks and the U.S. administration is notorious and helps solidify the close relationship, albeit claiming their independence, think tanks have with government (Bjorgaas 2012: 9).

The same report acknowledged it was necessary to pay for access to powerful politicians and bureaucrats in the U.S.: "Funding powerful think tanks are one way to gain such access, and some think tanks in Washington are openly conveying that they can service only those foreign governments that provide funding" (Bjorgaas 2012: 29). In other words, influence peddling is not a bug but a prerequisite of the system.

There are several examples of think tanks financed excessively by foreign interests to the extent that it creates a conflict of interest. Taiwan's generous financing of leading think tanks rarely receives much attention, despite the possible impact on U.S. policies related to China. The United Arab Emirates (UAE) paid the Center for a New American Security (CNAS) $250,000 for a report advocating the export of military drones to the UAE. A South Korean arms manufacturer, Hanwha Group, paid the Heritage Foundation $5.8 million to recommend the military hardware of their company (Clifton and Freeman 2021). The Heritage Foundation did not disclose their generous funding from Hanwha when opposing attempts by the international community to ban cluster ammunition, landmines, and automated weapons systems, which happened to be the weapons manufactured by Hanwha.

Think tanks such as the Atlantic Council publish endless articles on Russian interference in American democracy that strengthen the assumption that conflicts with Russia reflect a struggle between democracy and authoritarianism. Yet, these same think tanks receive huge amounts of funding from foreign governments with other causes to push. The Atlantic Council's financial report from 2019/2020 reveals that the financing from the UAE belonged to the "$1,000,000+" category together with contributors such as the British Foreign and Commonwealth Office, Facebook, Goldman Sachs, The Rockefeller Foundation, and other contributors (Atlantic Council 2020). It is impossible to prove conclusively the extent to which the funding impacts the analysis, yet a good indicator is the absence of its critical reporting on the UAE.

Russia has largely not bothered playing this game of funding American think tanks—perhaps because, mostly in the foreign policy and defense sectors, Moscow frequently serves as Enemy Number One for many advocacy groups.

The Ideology- and War-driven Idea Factories in the Post–Cold War Era

Think tanks market themselves as idea factories, and there was certainly a high demand for new ideas when the geopolitical realities of the Cold War came to an end and the world changed fundamentally. The bipolar international system was replaced with a unipolar system, and the political class was seeking new ideas to shape U.S. foreign policy and formulate new ideological positions. Concurrently, the military-industrial complex as the main funder of the think tanks had lost much of its business due to the end of the Cold War. Yet again, it was an opportune time for think tanks to shape U.S. post–Cold War policies.

Institutions have a tendency to live on after their initial purpose has ended, as a new raison d'etre is created to preserve the vast bureaucracy and influx of money. It was always unlikely that the huge military-industrial complex and think tanks would celebrate the new peace after the Cold War and reduce their size. Instead, they went looking for new monsters to slay.

Funding from an arms industry advocating for military solutions to shape the unipolar world united the competing ideologies of the political Left and Right. The neoconservatives aspired to perpetuate global hegemony while the neoliberals embraced the concept of humanitarian interventionism—two separate ideological rationalizations advancing the same foreign policy of "liberal hegemony."

Think tanks such as the Brookings Institute embraced humanitarian law in their advocacy for humanitarian interventionism around the world. Case in point: it was Ivo Daalder, a senior fellow at the Brooking Institution, who first argued strongly in favor of establishing an "Alliance of Democracies" as an alternative source of legitimacy parallel to international law under the UN. This liberal-democratic legitimacy, it was argued, would exempt the U.S. from international law, drawing a precedent from the invasion of Yugoslavia in 1999, and was needed to formalize legitimacy following the (illegal) invasion of Iraq (Daalder and Lindsay 2004). Thereafter, Daalder became the U.S. ambassador to NATO from 2009 to 2013. In 2017, a NATO-related NGO then named itself the Alliance of Democracies. If knowledge is power, then its corollary is: buy knowledge if you want to seize power.

At the same time as liberal think tanks were embracing the concept of humanitarian interventionism, a new militaristic neoconservatism also emerged. Neoconservative outfits such as the Project for a New American Century (PNAC) and the American Enterprise Institute (AEI) envisioned a hegemonic peace and gained immense influence, arguing that, without any other great powers, there would be no great power rivalry and that hegemony, therefore, was the route to peace—with the attendant advantage of legitimizing the expansion of U.S. influence and its subversion of independent poles of power. PNAC was founded in 1997 by William Kristol and Robert Kagan, two neoconservatives known for pushing an ideology that espouses the moral authority and virtue of U.S. militarism.

The influence of PNAC became evident when 10 out of the 25 people who signed under the founding principles of PNAC—Paul

Wolfowitz, Donald Rumsfeld, and Dick Cheney—ended up working for the administration of George W. Bush. Paul Wolfowitz is specifically tagged with having influenced the post-Cold War hegemonic ambitions of the U.S., with his Wolfowitz Doctrine (the unofficial name of the initial version of the Defence Planning Guidance document) leaked less than two months after the collapse of the Soviet Union. As Under Secretary of Defense for Policy Paul Wolfowitz, went on to develop the Defence Planning Guidance of February 1992, arguing that the primary objective of U.S. foreign policy should be to cement global dominance by preventing the rise of any future rivals: its "first objective is to prevent the re-emergence of a new rival" (DPG 1992).

PNAC subsequently became known as a think tank pushing an American imperial foreign policy that defined adversaries as threats by their mere capabilities to withstand U.S. power, irrespective of their intentions. Thus, think tanks contributed to advancing militaristic means in the pursuit of perpetual peace after the Cold War.

3. NATO and the Military Industrial Complex

Abraham Maslow wrote in 1966: "If the only tool you have is a hammer, it is tempting to treat everything as if it were a nail." Similarly, if military power is the main tool at their disposal, it is tempting for governments to pursue military solutions in response to all foreign policy problems. The U.S. could use a variety of tools, but diplomacy is not among them, with the Biden State Department itself pressing for arming (and rearmaing) Ukraine. Furthermore, huge commercial interests have invested heavily in the military option. The arms industry remains the dominant investor in the think tanks that influence U.S. foreign policy. The conflict of interest is blaring, as the suppliers of weapons have a commercial interest to create a demand for conflict.

U.S. military spending grows consistently to new heights, becoming a threat to the economic and financial stability of the U.S. However, its powerful arms industry that profits greatly from this reckless spending counters attempts to prevent imperial overstretch. This industry has deep pockets to fund doomsday narratives of security threats that can only be solved with more weapons.

It is no secret that arms manufacturers spend hundreds of millions every year to lobby politicians into making decisions that will profit them. Arms manufacturers flood Congress with campaign funding, and Congress sends the money of taxpayers back to the defense industry through more military spending. The think tanks have also obtained a privileged position at the money trough.

Pentagon contractors have become the main financers of think tanks as another form of lobbying. A report by the Foreign Influence Transparency Initiative revealed that defense contractors and government funds invested $1 billion in the top 50 most influential think tanks in the U.S. from 2014 to 2019 (Freeman 2020b). This means that every major think tank has an economic incentive to support all initiatives and narratives that involve military expansion. However, these think tanks insist that they are independent and reject any notion that there ight be a conflict of interest.

It was also revealed that 14 out of the 15 think tanks represented in House Armed Services Committee hearings between January 2020 and September 2022 had accepted money from the weapons industry (Semler 2022). Only the American Enterprise Institute (AEI) did not disclose receiving money from military contractors—because it does not disclose its donors. However, research into AEI reveals that they too are bought and paid for by weapon manufacturers. Conflict of interest is thus an understatement when the lobbyist for weapons manufacturers are the "experts" to advise on the need for more weapons.

A study in 2021 similarly reveals that nearly all major think tanks publishing reports on nuclear weapons are funded by companies involved in the nuclear weapons industry (ICAN 2021). The study revealed that the 21 corporations that received contracts in the production of nuclear weapons gave $10 million in grants to 12 think tanks in just one year. Furthermore, the CEOs of corporations involved in developing nuclear weapons sit on the advisory board of the Atlantic Council—which is known as the primary NATO think tank.

The Military Industrial Complex and NATO Expansion

President Dwight Eisenhower used his farewell speech in January 1961 to warn against the dangers of the "military-industrial complex." Eisenhower recognized that the Cold War with the Soviet Union had made it necessary to build an immense military industry. Building a war industry was nonetheless a new experience for the U.S., with great dangers to structures of governance. Eisenhower argued the U.S. had "been compelled to create a permanent armaments industry of vast proportions" to deal with security threats, but cautioned that "we must not fail to comprehend its grave implications." The implication was that the development of a huge industry that profited from war could potentially gain substantial independent political influence. Instead of the politicians requesting weapons from the arms manufacturers, a situation could emerge where the arms manufacturers requested wars from the politicians: "In the councils of government, we must guard against the acquisition of unwarranted influence, whether sought or unsought, by the military-industrial complex. The potential for the disastrous rise of misplaced power exists and will persist."

Eisenhower identified the corruption of the legislative branch as the main path to political influence for the arms manufacturers. In earlier drafts of the speech, Eisenhower had included Congress as a part of the problem as the renowned concept was first labeled the "military-industrial-congressional complex" (Roland 2021). However, as Eisenhower had already alienated too many military and political leaders by cautioning about the military-industrial complex, he decided not to provoke Congress by shaming their susceptibility to corruption by the arms industry.

The permanent militarization of the U.S. created deep structural changes in how the society, economy, and politics were organized. As the Cold War was coming to an end, none other than George Kennan warned about the dependence on the Soviet adversary to preserve U.S. militarism:

> Were the Soviet Union to sink tomorrow under the waters of the ocean, the American military-industrial complex would have to go on, substantially unchanged until some other adversary could be invented. Anything else would be an unacceptable shock to the American economy. (Cousins 1987: iv).

When the Cold War eventually came to an end along with the intense military rivalry, Kennan's theory could be tested. The end of the Cold War deprived the massive weapons industry of much of its funding, creating a shock to the U.S. economy.

NATO expansion offered a remedy to the declining need for weapons, and became the best hope of reviving the heydays of the military-industrial complex. New NATO members were required to upgrade their military equipment to be interoperable with other NATO states, which meant replacing the Soviet-era military systems of Central and Eastern Europe with American-made weapons. Subsequently, the arms industry became the leading ally of Clinton in promoting the expansion of NATO. As reported by *The New York Times* in March 1998, NATO expansion would be a bonanza for the military-industrial complex:

> American arms manufacturers, who stand to gain billions of dollars in sales of weapons, communication systems and other military equipment if the Senate approves NATO expansion, have made enormous investments in lobbyists and campaign contributions to promote their cause in Washington. (Seelve 1998)

Military contractors subsequently invested tens of millions of dollars in lobbying to advocate in favour of NATO expansion; it promised a return on investment in the tens of billions of dollars. The arms manufacturers provided generous contributions to both political parties, dwarfing other lobby activity from, for example, the tobacco industry.

A key driving force that supported NATO expansion was a group called the U.S. Committee to expand NATO, which was backed and directly led by the arms industry. The committee president, Bruce L. Jackson, was also the director of strategic planning for Lockheed. *The New York Times* reported:

> At night Bruce L. Jackson is president of the U.S. Committee to expand NATO, giving intimate dinners for Senators and foreign officials. By day, he is director of strategic planning

> for Lockheed Martin Corporation, the world's biggest weapons maker. (Gerth and Weiner 1997)

Insofar as the end of the Cold War produced great expectations and hopes for a durable peace, it was difficult for countries to combine the goal of sustainable peace and arming themselves to the teeth. Nonetheless, this became the official U.S. post-Cold War security strategy. Washington embraced the concept of hegemonic peace in which the overwhelming military power of the U.S. would discourage any great power rivalry. The U.S. National Security Strategy of 2002 explicitly linked military supremacy with peace, stating: "Our forces will be strong enough to dissuade potential adversaries from pursuing a military build-up in hopes of surpassing, or equaling, the power of the United States."

The problem is that unipolarity is inevitably a temporary condition, and attempting to achieve and perpetuate global hegemony only fuels great power rivalry. Sustaining unipolarity required the U.S. to prevent the emergence of rivals that could hope to surpass or equal the U.S. The effort to contain Russia and China as former Cold War rivals drove NATO expansion in Europe, and Obama's pivot to Asia once China became too big for the comfort of the U.S. One of the great political puzzles of the post-Cold War era is that every U.S. administration has insisted that they have embraced Russia and China, while Moscow and Beijing have consistently perceived the U.S. as continuing its containment policy.

Once these two great powers responded negatively to U.S. containment, the strategy of military supremacy was not reconsidered. Instead, the think tanks created an echo chamber, proclaiming that great power conflict was inevitable. A rising Russia and China meant rising profits for the arms manufacturers and the think tanks they fund, as long as Washington responded militarily to the new international distribution of power.

Think tanks played a crucial role in pushing the decision to expand NATO after the Cold War, which has been the most significant event shaping relations between the West and Russia. The U.S. was to a great extent divided on the issue of expanding NATO and think tanks worked hard to build up favorable support. They were often invited into briefings and their reports became an integral part of policy debate. Ronald Asmus (2003: 29), a Senior Transatlantic Fellow at the German Marshall Fund of the United States and Adjunct Senior Fellow at the Council of Foreign Relations, proudly asserted:

> There are moments in the evolution of U.S. foreign policy where think tanks have had a decisive impact in reshaping conventional wisdom and setting a new course on a key strategic issue. The debate over NATO enlargement in the early 1990s was one of those moments.

The political situation of the 1990s was favorable to think tanks. Europe was undergoing rapid revolutionary change, and there was an absence of expertise to deal with the situation. The absence of a clear status quo or established wisdom on a new security situation made it more susceptible to the expanding influence of think tanks:

> In the early 1990s RAND had one of the strongest teams of European security experts outside of the U.S. government. In addition to a close working relationship with different parts of the U.S. government, it also had excellent contacts in Western and Central and Eastern Europe as well as Russia. Along with the National Defense University and The Atlantic Council, it had been among the first think tanks on the ground in the new democracies of Central and Eastern Europe. Indeed, both the German as well as Central and East European governments had turned to these institutes to provide analytical support in developing new polices." (Asmus 2003: 30)

Further legitimacy was bestowed upon the think tanks by the testimonies of key officials such as Secretary of State Warren Christopher, Deputy Secretary of State Strobe Talbott, and U.S. Ambassador to the United Nations Richard Holbrooke, who all advocated for the important role of think tanks to inform on the decision of NATO expansion. They were far from strangers to them: Richard Holbrooke was periodically a board member of the Council on Foreign Relations (CFE) from 1993 to 2009, Warren Christopher was the vice chairman of the board of CFE from 1987 to 1991, and Strobe Talbott was the director of CFE from 1988 to 1993 before becoming president of the Brookings Institution from 2002 to 2017.

Ending the Negotiated Peace: Cancelling Pan-European Security Agreements

George Bush and Mikhail Gorbachev declared the Cold War to be over in 1989. and it had been agreed to construct a new inclusive European security architecture to replace the zero-sum rivalry between NATO and the Warsaw Pact. The Charter of Paris for a New Europe in 1990 outlined the basic principles for the new European security architecture, which entailed three important principles to negate the security dilemma: ending the dividing lines in Europe, embracing the principle of indivisible security in which "the security of every participating State is inseparably linked to that of all the others," and sovereign equality. These principles were reaffirmed with the Budapest Document in 1994, which established the Organisation for Security and Cooperation in Europe (OSCE) as an inclusive pan-European security institution.

The decision to expand NATO was drastic as it effectively entailed canceling these foundational agreements on pan-European security. The agreement to end the dividing lines in Europe was canceled and replaced as NATO's dividing lines gradually moved closer to Russian borders. The agreement of indivisible security was canceled as NATO increased its security at the expense of Russian security. Last, the agreement of sovereign equality was replaced with sovereign inequality as NATO relied on ideology to legitimize its hegemonic position. While presenting itself as the defender and champion of democracy and human rights, NATO in fact represented a system of liberal hegemony in which it claimed the prerogative to elevate itself above international law. In the alleged service of liberal values, it claimed NATO countries could legitimately interfere in the domestic affairs of other states, instigate coups, invade other countries, and change borders by force. In what became known as the "rules-based international system," NATO could excempt itself from international law by proclaiming to support liberal democracy and humanitarian law.

Think tanks were not only complicit in pushing for the abandonment of pan-European security agreements in favor of an international system based on "liberal hegemony"; they were also key in selling the message once it had been accepted. There are many early indications that the U.S. was determined to create a Europe without Russia, which entailed selling "European integration" as the rubric under which the decoupling from Europe's largest state, Russia, would be accomplished.

Case in point: one month after the collapse of the Soviet Union, President George H.W Bush delivered his State of the Union speech in which he triumphantly declared that "By the grace of God, America won the Cold War . . . we are the United States of America, the leader of the West that has become the leader of the world. " This statement was of immense importance as it represented a complete reversal from the former U.S. position that the Cold War had been negotiated to an end in 1989, which implied a common peace in a common Europe. In 1989, two years before the collapse of the Soviet Union, President Bush insisted that there should be no talk of "victory" and no dancing on the rubble of the Berlin Wall because the negotiated end of the Cold War meant "there were no losers, only winners" (Cohen 2009:160).

By switching the narrative from a negotiated settlement to a victory, Bush implied that post-Cold War Europe would be dictated by the victorious, without the participation of the loser. Jack Matlock (2010), the last U.S. Ambassador to the Soviet Union, cautioned against the dangerous "myth-making" about a U.S. victory in the Cold War, which unraveled the post-Cold War peace and created a more militaristic U.S. foreign policy due to the belief that peace was created through victory—not negotiations and diplomacy. The think tanks were an indispensable instrument towards this myth-making, which ensured a militaristic future for the U.S. to keep the war industry alive.

The fateful decision of expanding NATO was opposed by many leading thinkers in the U.S. George Kennan (1997), the architect of the containment policies against the Soviet Union, argued that "expanding NATO would be the most fateful error of American policy in the entire post-cold-war era." He lamented: "Why, with all the hopeful possibilities engendered by the end of the cold war, should East-West relations become centered on the question of who would be allied with whom." In an interview, Kennan further recognized that "There was no reason for this whatsoever. No one was threatening anybody else," and he predicted it would be "the beginning of a new cold war": "Of course there is going to be a bad reaction from Russia, and then [the NATO expanders] will say that we always told you that is how the Russians are—but this is just wrong" (Friedman 1998). Even known hawks, such as Richard Pipes, signed a statement by the Coalition Against NATO Expansion (CANE), which acknowledged the threat of NATO expansion:

> By its nature, a military alliance is directed against someone. The geography of NATO expansion makes its target clear: Russia... The proposal to expand NATO tosses it away by telling Russia in unmistakable terms that it remains excluded from the community of Western nations... [Russia] will remember, and ultimately, she will react, either from a position of renewed strength or out of desperation. The last great unfinished business of the 20th century is the reintegration of Russia with the West. With the proposal to expand NATO, we have turned our back on it. (CANE 1998).

Less than two weeks after NATO's first round of expansion in March 1999, NATO illegally attacked Yugoslavia. The implications for Russia were immense as it signified the end of NATO's status as a "defensive alliance," demonstrated that NATO would elevate itself above international law, and reinforced that by later recognizing Kosovo as an independent country the borders of Europe by military force for the first time since the Second World War. Aleksandr Solzhenitsyn, the prolific Russian author of *The Gulag Archipelago*, later recalled in an interview with *The New York Times* that the divorce between Russia and the West began with NATO's invasion of Yugoslavia:

> When I returned to Russia in 1994, the Western world and its states were practically being worshipped . . . This mood started changing with the cruel NATO bombings of Serbia. It's fair to say that all layers of Russian society were deeply and indelibly shocked by those bombings. The situation then became worse when NATO started to spread its influence and draw the ex-Soviet republics into its structure. This was especially painful in the case of Ukraine, a country whose closeness to Russia is defined by literally millions of family ties among our peoples, relatives living on different sides of the national border. At one fell stroke, these families could be torn apart by a new dividing line, the border of a military bloc (Neef and Schepp 2007).

NATO's Self-Preservation

Think tanks such as the Atlantic Council were devoted to sustaining NATO after the Cold War. As the Cold War ended, the alliance was an enormous and highly profitable organization. NATO employed thousands of people. People made careers in the organization. So why would they abolish them? As a result, NATO funds think tanks to keep the military alliance relevant, and it does so by hyping up perceived threats. This helped clear the path for its expansion and justify its continued existence, because the closer NATO moved to Russia's borders, the easier it became to spin Moscow as an adversary.

From the viewpoint of Russia, NATO appears to be an organization that exists to fight problems that are caused by its existence. Andrey Kortunov, Director General of the Russian International Affairs Council (RIAC), offers a reasonable take on why Russian foreign policy experts think the alliance continues. And, predictably, a lot of it comes down to money: "NATO's ineluctable enlargement has its own logic and justifications, or can at least be explained."

> One of these explanations is bureaucratic: each new member brings with it new personnel for the organization's executive office, new budgets and targeted projects, and new instruments of exerting administrative pressure on old members. One look at NATO's immense new headquarters, built two years ago at the cost of over $1 billion and taking up an area of over 250.000 square metres, is sufficient to understand why Brussels bureaucrats believe the enlargement process is rational. (Kortunov 2019).

Another explanation is legal: NATO cannot close its doors to potential new members without revising the 1949 North Atlantic Treaty, which states in Article 10 that NATO membership is open to "any other European State in a position to further the principles of this Treaty and to contribute to the security of the North Atlantic area." That is, NATO can reject specific applicants (the request of the Soviet Union was rejected in 1954, for example), but it cannot close its doors as a matter of principle. Revising or amending the founding Treaty under current circumstances is a purely hypothetical question.

A third explanation is economic: each subsequent candidate undertakes to modernize its weapons so that they comply with NATO standards. Accordingly, U.S. and European defense contractors gain a new market. It is not even important who ultimately pays for the modernization program, the candidate or the United States itself, since in any case, the enlargement of the organization means new contracts and new profits for its politically influential defense industry.

And finally, the political explanation: enlargement is one of the principal instruments of legitimizing NATO. The constant flow of candidates wishing to accede to NATO means that any talk of the alliance being obsolete, ineffective, or unneeded is moot. Enlargement is a weighty argument for those who disagree with the diagnosis recently made by the President of France, Emmanuel Macron, that NATO was experiencing "brain death."

As well as providing employment, Kortunov also believes NATO is an aid to career progression for elites, especially those from smaller states. "NATO has numerous national and international think tanks and leading European media outlets at its disposal," he observes. "Any ambitious politician from a Central European or Balkan country can clearly see that working in the NATO executive office may prove to be a unique springboard to a high-flying career. Suffice it to recall the story of Croatian Kolinda Grabar-Kitarović, who in 2015 moved from the office of Assistant Secretary-General of NATO for Public Diplomacy directly to the Presidential Palace in Croatia" (Kortunov 2019).

Richard Burt, a former Ronald Reagan staffer and former U.S. ambassador to Germany, argues that some of the poor decision-making of the 1990s concerning European security was caused by "a lobbying problem in NATO" (Majumdar 2018). Central and Eastern European countries also lobbied Washington and funded think tanks to push the agenda of moving the dividing lines eastward, as opposed to ending these dividing lines.

The expansion of NATO became an end in itself as think tanks such as the Atlantic Council worked tirelessly to formulate a post-Cold War purpose for the military bloc. Eastern European countries could also influence U.S. decision-making through NATO. Burt acknowledged that "Washington has become a bazaar. All of these countries want to influence our politics, so they all establish lobbying efforts and that does not lead to the most coherent decision making." He noted that attempting to include Georgia and Ukraine in NATO "was a bridge too far" and "We've been dealing with the consequences since then" (Majumdar 2018).

Former U.S. Secretary of Defence, Robert Gates (2014: 162), also recognized that NATO expansion had unraveled relations with Russia:

> When Russia was weak in the 1990s and beyond, we did not take Russian interests seriously. We did a poor job of seeing the world from their point of view, and of managing the relationship for the long term... The relationship with Russia had been badly mismanaged after Bush 41 left office in 1993. Getting Gorbachev to acquiesce to a unified Germany as a member of NATO had been a huge accomplishment. But moving so quickly after the collapse of the Soviet Union to incorporate so many of its formerly subjugated states into NATO was a mistake.... Trying to bring Georgia and Ukraine into NATO was truly overreaching.

However, the new democracies re-branding of NATO had created a new narrative for expansion that suggested NATO had transformed into an instrument for democratization. If Moscow opposed NATO expansion it implied that Russia rejected democracy, and NATO would then have to return to its original mission of containing Russia. Irrespective of how Russia responded, NATO would expand. The democratization rebranding in reality meant that NATO would be an insurance policy against future conflict with Russia. Secretary of State Madeleine Albright confirmed the insurance policy logic in a testimony to the Senate Armed Services Committee in April 1997: "On the off-chance that Russia doesn't work out the way that we are hoping it will... NATO is there" (Carpenter and Conry 1998). Former U.S. Secretary of State James Baker (2002) acknowledged that NATO had become "an insurance policy against resurgent and possibly virulent Russian nationalism." Baker warned against the approach of preparing NATO for a future conflict with Russia as it would become a self-fulfilling prophecy.

NATO's messaging to Russia was characterized by a contradictory approach of *reassurance* and *deterrence*. NATO reassured Russia it was not considered a threat and was not the target of NATO, although simultaneously deterring Russia by cautioning that NATO would be turned against Russia if it chose the wrong path. NATO (2010) defined this insurance policy thus: "because Russia's future policies toward

NATO remain difficult to predict, the Allies must pursue the goal of cooperation while also guarding against the possibility that Russia could decide to move in a more adversarial direction."

Missile Defence

Missile defence is a huge cash cow for the arms manufacturers, and thus of great interest to think tanks. As the American Enterprise Institute (AEI) acknowledges, think tanks had a key role in developing the ideas of missile defense and selling it to politicians and the public (AEI 2001).

Strategic missile defense systems are structured to intercept nuclear missiles. A missile defense system aimed against Russia cannot be considered to have *defensive* purposes because such a system would be overwhelmed by the huge amount of nuclear missiles that Moscow could launch against the U.S. in any first strike. Instead, a missile defense system aimed against Russia is inherently *offensive* as it is designed to intercept what would then be the limited second-strike capabilities of Russia with nuclear missiles that survived a U.S. first strike against Russia. In other words, missile defense can convert nuclear weapons into offensive weapons by intercepting the adversary's deterrent—its retaliatory capabilities.

None of this should be controversial, as the destabilizing nature of missile defense was the reason for signing the U.S.-Soviet Anti-Ballistic Missile Treaty (ABM-Treaty) in 1972. The Treaty banned strategic missile defense systems as it would disrupt the strategic balance between the two superpowers. In 1983, Ronald Reagan challenged the ABM-Treaty by calling for the development of the Strategic Defence Initiative (SDI), a missile defense system to defend against nuclear intercontinental ballistic missiles. The initiative represented nothing less than the repudiation of Mutually Assured Destruction (MAD), the idea that nuclear weapons have no offensive value when the other party's second-strike capabilities are sufficient to ensure the destruction of the attacker.

Reagan's interest in missile defense appears to have originated in 1979 when he realized how vulnerable the U.S. is in terms of its inability to defend itself from a Soviet attack. Reagan was mostly attracted to a proposal by General Daniel Graham to build a missile defense system to protect the U.S. from nuclear inter-continental ballistic missiles (Abelson 2014). In September 1981, Graham founded a think tank, High Frontier, to explore and promote the construction of missile defense. High Frontier ended up having a great influence on Reagan's decision to announce the Strategic Defence Initiative (missile defense) in March 1983. General Daniel Graham was a leading proponent for U.S. missile defense; he then became closely aligned with the Heritage Foundation and supporters in the Reagan administration.

Reagan's readiness to trust his experts and delegate decision-making to his subordinates presented important opportunities to think tanks that aimed to assert influence within his administration. Graham organized a group within the Heritage Foundation, using it as a sponsor to give them the infrastructure to develop research reports advocating the development of missile defense. As a key think tank of the 1980s, the Heritage Foundation gave Graham invaluable credibility and further access to the White House. It produced the report "High Frontier," prompting Reagan to write a letter of acknowledgment to Graham on 25 November 1985, stating: "I appreciate the important work that you and your colleagues have done to prepare the way for a more secure America. . . . I value greatly your continuing efforts to help us build a national consensus and to find the difficult answers for the profound strategic problems that face all of us in this nuclear age." In 1991, Reagan reiterated his attribution to Graham: "You and a small group of dedicated, determined people helped us move the SDI concept over all the roadblocks put up by people of less vision and belief in American capacity." Baker Spring (working at Heritage Foundation) noted that "basically our purpose in life at the Heritage Foundation was to debunk the national security value that was perceived with the policy of mutually assured destruction and, most specifically, to do things to get us out from under the AMB Treaty restrictions" (Abelson 2006: 194).

The idea of missile defense was revived as soon as the Soviet Union collapsed. One month after the collapse of the Soviet Union, President Bush, in his State of the Union speech, urged the legislators "to pass the Strategic Defense Initiative." Two months after the collapse of the Soviet Union, the aforementioned 1992 leaked Pentagon paper, Defence Planning Guidance, argued that in the post-Cold War world, Russia is "the only power in the world with the capability of destroying the United States," and called for an early introduction of a global anti-missile system (Tyler 1992).

Think tanks such as High Frontier, the Heritage Foundation, and the Center for Security Policy (CSP) were extremely influential in terms of promoting missile defense. The Project for a New American Century (PNAC), which had a domineering presence in the George W Bush administration, further pushed the idea of preparing the U.S. for multiple wars. Donald Rumsfeld (2003), PNAC member and U.S. Secretary of Defence, argued for a salami-tactics approach to missile defense:

> Instead of taking a decade or more to develop someone's vision of a "perfect" shield, we have instead decided to develop and put in place a rudimentary system by 2004—one which should make us somewhat safer than we are now—and then build on that foundation with increasingly effective capabilities as the technologies mature. We intend to apply this "spiral development" approach to a number of systems.

Engaging local think tanks was also a strategy for overcoming opposition to missile defense among European states. Case in point: Norway is an important partner in missile defense due to its Arctic geography, which is imperative to undermine Russia's retaliatory capabilities that would be launched across the north pole. Wikileaks (2007) revealed the cable "Norway: Missile Defence Public Diplomacy and Outreach," outlining how the U.S. embassy in Norway attempted to overcome opposition to missile defense by several means, including engaging with think tanks.

4. Spinning Russia

When it comes to Russia analysis and punditry, westerners can generally be defined into three categories: anti-Russian, moderate, and pro-Russia. That said, the latter term is often unfavorably stuck to people offering a balanced analysis, mainly because fair-handedness is considered an extreme position, given the narrow focus in which everything Russian is framed. The first speaks for itself, but the middle one has various layers. For instance, a person can be relatively even-handed but sympathetic to Russia's point-of-view or they can be somewhat neutral, but occasionally make a few hardline observations that contradict their usual middle-of-the-road bent.

As a rule, the former often have a steady academic post, or something similar, which gives them security and the freedom to maneuver. The second is customarily dependent on Western media, think tanks, or other NGOs for income. Indeed, privately, perhaps over a beer, this community will often concede that they are forced to stick to the "rules-of-the-game" even if they know better.

Almost inevitably, therefore, American and British establishments have tried to externalize blame for the worsening polarization in both countries. After all, it is the easy way out, and it buys the elites time before they will inevitably have to face up to the fallout from worsening domestic inequality, and the decline of the middle classes which were the bedrock of their political stability. However, the choice of Russia as the bogeyman, instead of, for example, China, which is more of a genuine rival, betrays how lazy and unimaginative western elites have become. Baby Boomers grew up with the specter of Soviet Communism as a credible threat to their way of life. The USSR was a vast empire, a political, economic, military, and technological superpower, which operated in a completely different system. Its mission was to trash the western capitalist model and replace it with its own totalitarian socialist version.

So blaming everything on "the Russians" is somewhat akin to rediscovering a childhood comfort blanket after decades of propaganda throughout the Cold War to shape the worldview. Sure, it's unimaginative, but it fits well, and it does not require much thought. A century ago, Lippmann argued that propaganda aims to develop social identities because "what matters is the character of the stereotypes" rather than the actual behavior of the targeted countries (Lippman 1922: 70). Human beings find comfort in these stereotypes and instinctively reject any information that disrupts this comfort blanket: "No wonder then, that any disturbance of the stereotypes seems like an attack upon the foundations of the universe. It is an attack upon the foundations of our universe" (Lippmann 1922: 52).

The fact is that everything that helps to boost Western polarisation is produced and consumed by Westerners themselves. Blaming this stuff on external actors has become an industry, with one anti-Russia think tank, Atlantic Council, seeing its annual revenue grow by ten times in the past decade. It's hardly a surprise that this pressure group's big theme in recent years has been "disinformation," even creating a stand-alone cut-out, known as the Digital Forensic Research Lab (DFRL), to keep the scare stories coming (*New York Times* 2016).

It also specializes in smearing anti-establishment figures as Russian "assets." "Why is Tulsi Gabbard still in the democratic presidential race? Who has not understood that she is a Kremlin stooge?" tweeted Atlantic Council fellow Anders Aslund in February 2020. "Who finances her? Dark money? I could guess its source." This is just one example of this sort of thing. But what makes it stunning is that the think tank is funded by various U.S. government agencies. So, you had a lobbyist from a partially state-bankrolled institution telling his thousands of followers that a U.S. presidential candidate, and army veteran, was working for Moscow. This is the new normal.

What makes it more staggering is that it's a mirror image of how the U.S. is viewed in Russian public mythology, where whenever something bad happens, it tends to be blamed on the Americans. The difference is the U.S. has long positioned itself as being above that kind of discourse. It was, after all, supposed to be the "shining city on the hill."

In reality, the Russia of the 1990s was not a U.S. competitor to anywhere near the same extent as its erstwhile predecessor. While Russia retained some of the military and scientific advantages it inherited from the Soviet Union, it was not even the biggest economy in Europe, let alone a global financial superpower. In the spring of 2020, Russian GDP was neck and neck with that of Germany, measured by purchasing power parity (PPP), and in nominal U.S. dollars, it was only fifth, also behind Britain, France, and Italy. By a much-bruited Western meme: Russia was a "gas station parading as a country." What's more, over the past thirty years, it had become fully integrated into the American-led Western financial and trade organism. The superrich had properties in London and Florida. Companies such as Mcdonald's and IKEA became ubiquitous across the country and Russia takes part in the World Trade Organisation, the Council of Europe, and all sorts of supranational bodies. In other words, Russia itself became part of the broader West.

In the 1990s, there was even something of a friendship between the two elites, albeit based on a core-periphery, subject/object or teacher/student dynamic. If the Kremlin had continued to accept that America, as the cold war "victor," called the shots, the friendship could even have continued.

European integration and the subsequent military, political and economic structures after the Cold War were organized along what can be referred to as "inter-democratic security institutions" (Diesen 2015). The West attempted to accommodate Russia as a civilizational object, envisioning a socializing role for itself with relations with Russia organized as a subject-object / teacher-student relationship.

Russia would not have a seat at the table, rather its participation in international security was to be largely limited to improving its governance per Western precepts. The unipolar format in Europe necessitated a perpetually weak Russia that would abide by institutions that did not grant Moscow representation. Cooperation between a teacher and a student does not entail compromise and mutual social learning, rather it was for the Russian student to accept unilateral concessions, with decisions made unilaterally by the West and implemented by Russia. Instead of referring to Russian security interests and policies, there was a pedagogic language with references to Russian "behavior" that should be modified with "rewards" or "punishment."

Collective bargaining power became maximized with NATO+1 and EU+1 relationships. Both the EU and NATO assigned themselves a pedagogic role aimed to socialize Russia (Neumann 1999: 107–9; Browning 2003: 58; Zürn and Checkel 2005: 1056; Gheciu 2005). Implicit in the teacher-student format is the assumption that Russia, as a political object, accepts one-sided adjustments and unilateral concessions. By conflating Western values with its national interests, Russia can be included to the extent it abides by the decisions of the West, thus making Russia responsible for its own exclusion if it does not embrace its role as a political object (Möller 2003: 316).

In NATO's view, Russia could accept a new international order of U.S. global hegemony or be punished. The dilemma this posed for Russia became imminent with NATO's expansion, forcing it to face the prospect of either accepting its role as an eternal apprentice of the West and supporting the creation of a European security architecture that marginalized Moscow, or resisting it and being castigated as a counter-civilizational force (Williams and Neumann 2000).

Russia was weak in that decade; the economic transition from communism did so much damage that average wages dropped to about $100 monthly if they were paid at all. The country was reliant on IMF bailouts, and even various forms of aid, and its longevity had dropped by a decade. Nevertheless, it did attempt Western integration, even joining the G8, cooperating with NATO, and bringing in various foreign advisors to reform its way of doing things. Alas, two events sowed doubts about whether the country was on the right road: The first financial and the second, geopolitical.

In 1998, Russia went bankrupt, defaulting on its debts. The resultant crisis was another kick in the teeth after a decade of following a Western course. Then the following year NATO expanded without including Russia, and bombed Russia's "brotherly ally," Serbia, another Orthodox Christian European state. Foreign Minister Yevgeny Primakov was so disgusted, he turned his plane around while on the way to New York. Russia was on its knees, and clearly, something had to change. The state was being controlled by a cabal of oligarchs, with the vast majority of ordinary people living in penury.

Enter Putin

Yeltsin's pro-Western political platform was based on the assumption that unilateral concessions toward the West would be rewarded with the inclusion of Russia into a Greater Europe. When NATO expanded and invaded Yugoslavia in 1999, the entire political platform of Yeltsin collapsed. Thus, Yeltsin and his clique decided on Vladimir Putin as his successor. Now, whatever your feelings about Putin—and globally they range from incredible admiration for him to absolute hatred of all he stands for—the facts are that Russia's economy has grown substantially under his leadership and the country has been stabilized. Indeed, given the extent of the malaise in 1999, the turnaround was relatively swift.

Problems erupted when Moscow awoke from its stupor and rejected any further unilateral concessions. First, Putin refused to support the illegal 2003 U.S./UK-led invasion of Iraq. However, because France and Germany also strongly objected, it did not become a wedge issue at that point. After this, NATO expansion increased and in 2009 President Nicholas Sarkozy took France back into the U.S.-led alliance's command structure, which served to further differentiate Russia from the rest of Europe.

Propaganda involves demonizing the political leadership of an adversarial state as the complexity of national security issues are reduced to the personal characteristics of leaders to facilitate public consumption. Focusing the narrative on the criminal nature or deficient mental condition of a state leader is appealing as it distracts from more serious discourse about conflicts deriving from competing for security interests. Instead, all conflicts are reduced to a rivalry between good and evil. Putin is routinely portrayed by the West as thuggish, brutal, a bully, a gangster, and other inferences of criminality and illegitimacy. A more recent development over recent years is also to depict the Russian president as suffering from mental illness. The Office of Net Assessment (ONA), which describes itself as an internal Pentagon think tank, speculates that Putin has Asperger's syndrome, "an autistic disorder which affects all of his decisions." This "profound handicap" of Asperger's means that Putin is at a "primitive," "pre-mammalian" and "reptilian stage of development" (Schrad 2015).

5. Atlantic Council: NATO's Propaganda Wing

The Atlantic Council is an important think tank to explore due to its close affiliation with NATO, and because of its rapid increase in funding. In the decade from 2006–2016, its annual revenue grew from $2 million to $21 million, a more than a ten-fold increase. It's important to mention this incredible rise because it happened during a time when think tanks started to attract funds normally pushed toward straight-up lobbying firms. Indeed as U.S. Senator Elizabeth Warren noted, giant corporations "figured out that by spending, hey, a few tens of millions of dollars, if they can influence outcomes here in Washington, they can make billions of dollars" (Lipton 2013).

The Atlantic Council's funding is almost as global as the soccer World Cup. It brings in so much money that it lists its backers by financial bracket, much like how Catholic priests once read out donations during mass to encourage parishioners to show their devotion. Supplying more than a million dollars, annually, are the British Foreign Office, the Embassy of the United Arab Emirates in Washington, and Saudi billionaire Bahaa Hariri. In the 500,000 to a million band, you find Moroccan (OCP Foundation), Ukrainian (System Capital Management), and Swedish (The Wallenberg Foundations) cash, alongside a generous contribution from the U.S. State Department. Next up is $250,000–$500,000, where more money comes from UAE (Abu Dhabi National Oil Company, Mubadala Development, and Crescent Petroleum), in addition to the Netherlands (Airbus), Turkey

(Çalik Holdings, MNG Group, and Limak Holdings), Britain (HSBC), Moldova (Trans Oil), Ukraine (Viktor Pinchuk) and Poland (PKO). Meanwhile, South Korea, Denmark, and Sweden drop direct state funds into the pot.

Next comes the $100,000–$249,000 division. And here we have Brazilian, British, Polish, Ukrainian (including from notorious gas company "Burisma" where Hunter Biden obtained a position after the coup in 2014), Japanese, Italian, Emirati, Sudanese, South Korean, Spanish, Hungarian, Norwegian, Swiss and Romanian funding.

Now, one could argue that these foreign interests are pouring money into the Atlantic Council for altruistic reasons such as the desire to support important unbiased research. However, the more likely answer is that they are doing it for reasons of access, prestige, or influence. When it comes to influencing the press agenda, the Atlantic Council is arguably the most successful think tank. Its lobbyists are ubiquitous across the information space, and it has also been remarkably successful in its embrace of social media and online publishing.

Furthermore, the pressure group's ability to attract "big names" to events and outreach projects is second to none. Even if that means resorting to plenty of morally dubious calls. For instance, in 2018, the Atlantic Council presented ex-U.S. President George Bush with its "Distinguished Leadership Award." Notably, Bush forgot to mention the word "Iraq" is his acceptance speech. This is a bit like Buzz Aldrin turning up to an event where he does not bother talking about the moon—while facing an audience happy not to raise the subject.

The Atlantic Council originated in the early years of NATO, which was founded in 1949 with an initial twelve members. Five years later, the Atlantic Treaty Organisation was established to support the American-led military alliance, with a remit to bring together diplomats, academics, military leaders, and politicians to support the U.S.-led alliance. The Atlantic Council is a member of this umbrella body.

The Atlantic Council is a fierce advocate for NATO and berates the notion that this military alliance could in any way be considered a threat to Russia. Yet, the Atlantic Council has also advocated war against Russia. Evelyn Farkas (2022), a senior Fellow at the Atlantic

Council, and also former U.S. deputy assistant secretary of defense for Russia, Ukraine, and Eurasia in the Obama administration, and former senior advisor to the Supreme Allied Commander in NATO, penned an op-ed titled "The U.S. Must Prepare for War Against Russia over Ukraine," in which she argued that point. This was not a reference to a defensive war, but for an offensive war to push back Russia:

> We must not only condemn Russia's illegal occupations of Ukraine and Georgia, but we must demand a withdrawal from both countries by a certain date and organize coalition forces willing to take action to enforce it. . . . The horrible possibility exists that Americans, with our European allies, must use our military to roll back Russians—even at the risk of direct combat.

In terms of its core mission, the Atlantic Council is best described as "NATO's propaganda wing," and its principal agenda remains the same today: keep the Americans in Europe, and the Russians out. However, its decades of campaigning have also proven useful in another way because they have allowed the Atlantic Council to build a superb network which, quite evidently, a lot of wealthy donors are keen to access.

As documented, back in 1998, by Melvin Small (1998), now "distinguished professor of history emeritus" at Wayne State University in Detroit, right from the start, the Atlantic Council was more about networking than policy formation. It was "a center for informal get-togethers for prominent visiting Europeans" whose directors were "generally satisfied to act behind the scenes, promoting their ideas and not their institution."

Throughout the Cold War, its directors included "virtually all former (U.S.) Secretaries of State and scores of prominent diplomats." In other words, the Atlantic Council has always been about influence peddling and "information warfare." And the Internet age has suited it down to the ground. Today one of its obsessions is "disinformation" which it is fond of spreading, itself, while attempting to frame that activity as unique to "enemies" of NATO.

On 17 May 2018, Facebook announced its partnership with the Atlantic Council and the Atlantic Council's Digital Forensic Research Lab. The main objective of the partnership was to "fight disinformation" as Facebook was stepping up censorship on its platform. Facebook has already established a partnership with two other major think tanks to deal with disinformation—the International Republican Institute (IRI) and the National Democratic Institute (NDI), both funded by the U.S. government through the National Endowment for Democracy. From the onset, Facebook has chosen some questionable partners to run its Ministry of Truth.

The Atlantic Council has a profoundly troubled and strange history with disinformation, as this chapter will outline. For instance, in June 2018, its lobbyist Alexander Vershbow recorded a bizarre video, where he claimed the very concept of "disinformation" was uniquely Russian and the term itself was of Russian origin. "The word 'disinformation' comes from the Russian language . . . 'dezinformatsiya,'" he claimed. "It was pioneered by the KGB and Joseph Stalin." However, Vershbow's very statement was "disinformation" because the word is not Russian in origin. It was borrowed from the Polish language in the 18th century. Which itself had taken it from the Latin word, *informatio.* And the concept was not created in Russia, either. Now, if it were some greenhorn intern you could laugh about it. But Vershbow is a man with serious credentials, including four years as Deputy Secretary-General of NATO and a similar length of time as U.S. Ambassador to Russia.

Cases like these expose how think tanks raise the "disinformation alarm" selectively and are often guilty of the practice themselves. Its lobbyists are also keen to shut down voices that disagree with the outfit's agenda, often resorting to slurs and smears. Think tanks create stories and experts that are offered on a plate for journalists, which are the main source for influence in the media. However, in order to shape the narrative, think tanks such as the Atlantic Council are also in the business of crushing dissent.

Crushing Dissent: The Case of "@Ian56789"

In March 2018, the Atlantic Council's Ben Nimmo, himself a former NATO press officer, produced a report on "pro-Kremlin trolls," whom he accused of "organized activity" to sow confusion on Twitter. It came in the aftermath of the alleged poisoning in Salisbury, England of the Skripals: Sergei, a Russian-born spy who defected to England, and his daughter, Yulia. Nimmo himself is an interesting case. He has managed to become ubiquitous across Western media as a "disinformation expert," despite having no obvious qualifications to justify the title. At the same time, his background (and indeed backing) is rarely explained to readers, listeners or viewers. Instead, he's usually presented as some sort of neutral voice. This is a bit as if reporters during the 2003 U.S./UK invasion of Iraq were to describe the infamous "Comical Ali" as a freelance journalist based in Baghdad.

Nimmo identified "@Ian56789" as a "Kremlin-troll," which was meant to insinuate the user was based in St Petersburg or elsewhere in Russia, and was attempting to maneuver British public opinion to suit Moscow's agenda. A few weeks later the account was suspended by Twitter, in a move Nimmo publicly celebrated. However, the info warrior's credibility took a severe blow when the man behind the handle unmasked himself, live on Sky News.

"@Ian56789" was Ian Shilling, a middle-aged, "ordinary British citizen," given to conducting his own independent research on issues. Shilling felt he was being targeted due to his non-mainstream views on major stories. Thus, a British subject had been smeared as a sort of Russian agent, by an "expert" from a think tank partially funded with UK taxpayer's money. It was a story which, in normal circumstances, one would imagine the UK press would plaster all over.

However, today, traditional media outlets are more-or-less uniformly pro-NATO. With even the *Guardian*, once a hotbed of alternative viewpoints, now as supportive of U.S./UK foreign policy objectives as the *Times* or *Telegraph*. The lack of kickback seemed to embolden Nimmo. Instead of apologizing, the think tanker doubled down. "Interesting to see the real face of Ian56789, rather than the David Gandy one, at last. Not a troll factory account. Rather, a pro-Kremlin troll (definition based on [the] use of someone else's picture, systematic use of Kremlin narratives, and repetitive abusive behavior)."

At this point, Wikileaks stepped in, tweeting from its official account, "you literally produced, with money from weapons companies and dictatorships, a fake news story that spread all over the world, defaming a very British retiree, who wants to reduce arms company profits, as a Kremlin bot. So who's the paid troll?." This tweet would become even more on point a year later when Nimmo's involvement with the British government's "Integrity Initiative," became known, which is something we will discuss later.

The think tanker's methodology for deciding who merits the tag "Kremlin bot" or "Kremlin troll" is rather bizarre. What gives the intruder's game away, according to Nimmo, is the use of imperfect English. For instance, he cited the "inability" to properly use "a" or "the" in sentences, because the Russian language does not use definite or indefinite articles (RT 2018a).

This sort of attitude to criticism is typical of Atlantic Council lobbyists. When faced with alternative views, they either block or smear. Nimmo's diatribe about alleged "Kremlin Trolls" did not only focus on Ian Shilling. It also defamed others, including world-renowned Ukrainian-American pianist Valentina Lisitsa and Maram Susli, a Syrian living in Perth, Australia (RT 2018b). The latter, who tweets as @Partisangirl, was vilified as a "Russian bot" by a number of UK media outlets. She claims the slander was based on research from Nimmo, and also noted how Atlantic Council was then partially funded by the "Syria Campaign," the same outfit behind the well-known "White Helmets" group, also recipients like George Bush of a "Freedom Award" from Atlantic Council. The "Syria Campaign's" primary sponsor is Britain's Asfari Foundation.

The lengths to which U.S./UK mainstream media goes to promote Nimmo are also rather bizarre. In February 2020, *The New York Times* published a long hagiography, replete with "lifestyle" photos of him near his Scottish home (Satariano 2020). The piece, written by Adam Satariano, did briefly mention his work with NATO, but presented it in an "inspiring" way. The newspaper labeled him "a leader of a small but growing community of online sleuths" as if he were doing it for the hell of it.

Here is an incredible line from the article: "he moved to Scotland to be closer to family and began doing contract work on Russia for pro-democracy think tanks like the Institute for Statecraft." Of course, *The New York Times* mentions nothing about the scandals involving that Institute, or the fact it was essentially an information warfare operation, run by the British government. "During the 2016 American election campaign, Mr. Nimmo helped found the Atlantic Council's Digital Forensic Research Lab, a Washington-based group that studies online disinformation," Satariano then writes, again not mentioning the fact the Atlantic Council is essentially NATO's propaganda wing and is also heavily funded by the UK state.

Now imagine if someone was working for think tanks funded by the Russian government. You can bet your life it would be the main focus of the story, let alone a line dropped in somewhere. There is also the revelation that "Facebook made him and the [Atlantic Council] lab among the first outsiders allowed to study disinformation networks on its site before the company shut the networks down." That should scare anyone who uses the social network. But, then again, by now, Facebook users are probably aware that anything they do there might as well be put on a postcard and left on a bar counter.

The New York Times does let its readers know that the "Digital Forensic Research Lab has received funding from Facebook" but neglects to mention all the other backers of the Atlantic Council.

A lack of self-awareness is common among ideologues. And Nimmo is not alone at the Atlantic Council, in this regard. The organization is permeated with folk who will not tolerate other points of view, even from genuine experts, although its efforts to censor and cancel are commonly disguised and legitimized under the auspices of fighting disinformation.

Blacklisting the Kremlin's Trojan Horses

The Atlantic Council produced a series of publications under the title the "Kremlin's Trojan Horses," which are blacklists to shame and criminalize politicians, journalists, experts, and political parties for being too friendly towards Russia. The criteria for being designated a Russian Trojan horse were criticism of NATO, advocacy of reducing anti-Russian sanctions, or expressing understanding for Russian actions.

It is worth exploring those who are denounced as the Kremlin's Trojan Horses, as it becomes evident that many of the political parties, academics, and journalists are not actually friendly to Russia; rather their crime is not being sufficiently hawkish. The European political parties alone that are listed as the Kremlin's Trojan horses include the UK's Labour and UKIP; Germany's Die Linke and Alternative for Germany; France's Republicans and National Front; The Netherlands' Freedom Party and Forum for Democracy; Belgium's Flemish Interest; Austria's Freedom Party of Austria; Italy's Lega Nord and Democratic Party; Hungary's Fidesz and Jobbik; Greece's Syriza and Golden Dawn; Bulgaria's Ataka; the Czech Republic's Workers Party for Social Justice and The Czech Communist Party; Lithuania's Order and Justice Party; Sweden's Sweden Democrats; Norway's Progress Party, Socialist Left Party, and Red Party; Denmark's People's Party; and Spain's Podemos (Atlantic Council 2016, 2017, 2018). The Atlantic Council calls for "exposing" their opaque connections in what can be interpreted as an effort to delegitimize and blacklist the political opposition.

Oystein Bogen, the journalist who wrote the Norwegian blacklist for the Atlantic Council, also wrote a hit piece on the author of this book. The journalist did not inform his readers about his work for the Atlantic Council to smear and blacklist Norwegian politicians, academics, and journalists. The political parties smeared by Bogen would be surprised to be labelled pro-Russian as their crimes appeared to not be suffiently anti-Russian. In the article, Bogen (2021) in McCarthyite tradition warns about an ominous enemy among us, a professor who allegedly spreads Russian propaganda from a Norwegian university.

Remarkably, the article did not contain a single example of incorrect evidence or a flawed argument to substantiate the accusation of propaganda. Much like his contribution, the purpose of other contributors to the Atlantic Council's Kremlin's Trojan Horses series is to attack, shame, and cancel people with opposing perspectives by portraying them as traitors. In the twisted logic of these think tanks and their collaborators in the media, they are defending democracy by cleansing society of criticism of NATO or failing to advocate for hardline policies against Russia.

The Case of Bellingcat, the Atlantic Council's Digital Forensic Partner

Bellingcat can be considered a branch of the Atlantic Council insofar as the founder of Bellingcat also works for the Atlantic Council, and both organizations receive money from many of the same sources. Bellingcat is a natural fit for the Atlantic Council as Bellingcat is also an organization devoted to the information war against Russia, while presentong itself as an independent organization. More specifically, Bellingcat sells itself as an independent investigative organization by branding itself as "an intelligence agency for the people," although it is largely a government intelligence agency masquerading as private and using independent citizen journalists to obtain credibility.

Bellingcat was established by Eliot Higgins, a self-proclaimed eager video gamer. Higgins admitted in an interview with the *Guardian*: "I knew no more about weapons than the average Xbox owner. I had no knowledge beyond what I'd learned from Arnold Schwarzenegger and Rambo" (Waever 2013).

Higgins began his rise to fame by "studying" pictures on social media of the gas attack in the Ghouta suburb in Syria in August 2013. The media, searching for any evidence that could substantiate the conclusions and narratives of a rogue Assad regime gassing his own people, uncritically celebrated the findings of the blogger as conclusive evidence. However, in the world of real experts, there was less enthusiasm for Higgins's "investigation." His findings of the Syrian government's culpability were later debunked by journalists and weapons experts. Theodore Postol, a professor at the Massachusetts Institute of Technology, and former UN weapons inspector Richard Lloyd conducted an extensive forensic report of the Ghouta attack that reached the conclusion the missiles were launched from a rebel-controlled region (Lloyd and Postol 2014). When asked about the research conducted by Higgins, Postol responded that he "has done a very nice job collecting information on a website. As far as his analysis, it's so lacking any analytical foundation it's clear he has no idea what he's talking about" (Russell-Sluchansky 2014). Nonetheless, in a media landscape where the right conclusions matter the most, Higgins rose to fame.

The next great achievement of the media's favorite blogger was his investigation of MH17, the Malaysian passenger flight that was shot down over Eastern Ukraine in July 2014. Yet again, the media was in search of evidence that would prove Russian culpability and Higgins could deliver. Higgins / Bellingcat used digital forensic software to conclude that Russia manipulated images on Photoshop.

However, in the real world, the findings were dismissed by experts as Higgins was an amateur who did not know how to use the software. Actual forensic experts denounced the report by Bellingcat as an "erroneous interpretation," as the alleged evidence "doesn't prove anything" (Bidder 2015). *Spiegel Magazine* revealed that Higgins did not use the digital analytical tools correctly and his evidence was dismissed as "doing is nothing more than reading tea leaves. Error Level Analysis is a method used by hobbyists" (Bidder 2015).

When confronted with his shortcomings, Higgins would commonly respond by stating "suck my balls." Despite the unprofessional demeanor of the blogger, his lack of relevant skillset, failure in using digital forensic tools, and reaching the wrong conclusion—the media was attracted by his ability to provide purported evidence for their allegations. Here, the think tanks and intelligence agencies figured, was a potential partner in the information against Russia.

In 2016, Higgins was hired as a senior fellow in the Atlantic Council's Digital Forensic Research Lab and Future Europe Initiative projects. The funding for Bellingcat also poured in through funding from the National Endowment for Democracy. In an article written in the Atlantic Council, Higgins (2016) defined Bellingcat as an instrument against Russia titled "New generation of digital detectives fight to keep Russia honest." Far from only providing the "research," Higgins also began publishing policy recommendations in the Atlantic Council that included containing Russia and launching air strikes against Syrian government soldiers (Czuperski et.al. 2016).

Over the next years, Bellingcat seemingly replaced the need for Western intelligence agencies as the investigations by Higgins took over exposing all the evil of Russia—including the alleged poisoning of the Skripals in 2018 and of Navalny in 2020. Leaked documents show how Bellingcat collaborates with the UK Foreign and Commonwealth Office, which funds various media outlets to change attitudes and to "weaken the Russian state's influence" (Maté 2021). A leaked note from the Integrity Initiative, funded by the British Foreign Office, acknowledged that Bellingcat's credibility as a source was diminishing: "Bellingcat was somewhat discredited, both by spreading disinformation itself, and by being willing to produce reports for anyone willing to pay" (Maté 2021).

Marc Polymeropolous, the CIA's former deputy chief of operations for Europe and Eurasia, was explicit about the usefulness of Bellingcat for U.S. intelligence agencies: "Whenever we had to talk to our liaison partners about it, instead of trying to have things cleared or worry about classification issues, you could just reference their work" (Mackinnon 2020). Daniel Fried, a retired U.S. diplomat also hailed the unique function of Bellingcat: "The advantage of having Bellingcat do it is that you don't have to have to have a sources-and-methods debate within your government" (Mackinnon 2020). While the CIA celebrates the role of Bellingcat as an instrument against Russia, they insist that there is no direct cooperation.

In April 2018, Canadian journalist Aaron Maté attempted to set up a debate between Eliot Higgins from the Atlantic Council / Bellingcat, and Theodore Postol, professor emeritus of Science, Technology, and International Security at MIT (RT 2018c). Higgins turned down the challenge, dismissing the renowned academic as an "idiot." This was quite something to say about a man who once worked as a scientific adviser to the chief of naval operations at the Pentagon. Especially given Higgins himself has no recognized scientific qualifications.

To be fair, a debate did take place later. The two locked horns the following autumn, at the Center for Investigative Journalism's Conspiracy conference in London. And, predictably, the debate was bitter, with both accusing the other of covering up genocide. "I think that Ted's work is a disgrace. It's being used to deny war crimes," Higgins insisted. "And I think it's absolutely disgusting." "You fabricate the data and arguments," replied Postol. "You are essentially causing people, who might have committed a war crime, to go free" (RT 2018d).

The Social Media/ Media Connection

In the age of social media, we can often see attempts to spread disinformation in real time from think tanks to the media. Case in point: in May 2018, Atlantic Council lobbyist Agnia Grigas tweeted: "Russia's economy needs to be 70% larger to meet its target of being a top 5 world economy by 2024. The IMF predicts that Russia's position will not change before 2023." Now, first off, her message was misinformation. She was referring to various statements by Vladimir Putin, where he expressed the desire to break into the top quintet. The purpose of her tweet was apparently to portray Putin's objective as being outlandish and out of reach. But the Russian President referred to the objective of being the world's fifth largest economy measured by purchasing power parity (PPP). At the time of her post, the World Bank already ranked Russia as the world's sixth largest economy measured by PPP, placing it only $150 billion behind the German economy (*Moscow Times* 2018). Russia therefore did not have much catching up to do, with a marginal improvement in fortunes, or a deterioration in Germany, sufficient to move up the table. Was Grigas not aware of why PPP is commonly used as a better indicator than GDP? Was the mistake caused by ignorance or malice?

Either way, what's interesting is how Grigas amplified her message. She tagged fellow Atlantic Council lobbyist Anders Aslund (who has a large social media following), as well as Mike Gonzalez of "Hermitage;" Joe Biden-advisor, and consistent Russia-critic, Michael Carpenter; and Jaana Remes of "McKinsey" and the Jamestown Foundation. But, far more interestingly, she added two journalists, the U.S. editor of the *Financial Times,* Peter Spiegel, and Valentina Romei, a journalist from the same newspaper. Obviously, the lobbyist tagged the reporters so the post would come to their attention, which is something PR people do daily. But when the assertion is disinformation, well, that raises numerous ethical issues. And gives an additional small insight into Atlantic Council's methods.

All this media outreach by the Atlantic Council yields results, and there are plenty of examples. But here are two from 2019: Luke Harding, a former *Guardian* correspondent in Moscow, publicly thanked the Atlantic Council for feeding him a silly story about how "suspected Russian spies" allegedly spread a fake plot to assassinate (British Prime Minister) Boris Johnson on social media. "Me in the Observer on Moscow's latest online influence operation." he tweeted. "Fake Russian stories include a 'plot' by Remainers to kill Boris Johnson and a claim that novichok used against Sergei Skripal came from (the) Real IRA . . . thanks Ben Nimmo."

Nimmo was busy that week because only four days later, the *Times* ran a very similar story. Except for this time, the angle was "a Russian operation tried to reignite the Troubles with fake stories claiming that the DUP is open to Irish reunification and the Real IRA is recruiting Islamist fighters," as reported by Mark Bridge. Here, the Atlantic Council is described as a "Washington Think Tank," again with leaders left none the wiser about its agenda or funding.

With journalism in crisis as budgets tighten, think tank lobbyists can essentially hand under-pressure hacks ready-made tales. And as long as they keep getting away with it, plenty will play along, safe in the knowledge that nobody in mainstream media is scrutinizing the Atlantic Council, However, if they did, they might have second thoughts about the company it keeps.

Promoting "Freedom" in Former Soviet Republics

The Atlantic Council is an eager supporter of Washington's efforts to promote anti-Russian sentiments in former Soviet republics. These efforts are sold as spreading democracy and freedom, although in reality, they reflect crude geopolitics. The pressure groups' use of former Soviet states to push its anti-Russian line is worthy of a chapter in itself, but this book can't overdose on one topic, making it as one-note as most of the organizations it covers. So, let's just offer a few brief examples.

The Atlantic Council has supported Ukraine in decoupling its cultural and linguistic ties from Russia at all costs. It ignores all possible religious issues by celebrating Ukraine's decoupling from the Russian Orthodox Church as an important step towards sovereignty. This laid the foundation for Ukraine to purge the Orthodox Church in 2022 and expulsion of Orthodox monks. Furthermore, the Atlantic Council argues in favor of Ukrainian nation-building and "cultural revival" based on purging Russian culture from Ukraine:

> Thanks to centuries of political domination and systematic russification, modern Russia still enjoys enormous cultural influence over independent Ukraine. When hostilities began seven years ago, this became a matter of national security. . . . The Ukrainian authorities have also embraced a number of protectionist policies in order to restrict Russia's soft power penetration inside Ukraine. In 2014, Ukraine banned a range of Russian TV channels, TV series, and books. . . . Three years later, Ukraine went further and blocked a number of Russian social media platforms. Many of Russia's leading pop stars and celebrities are also no longer welcome in Ukraine. (Pesenti 2021).

In July 2018, the Atlantic Council even invited a Ukrainian politician with deep ties to neo-Nazi groups as a speaker, one Andriy Parubiy. He appeared at an event titled "The Frontlines of Freedom: A

Conversation with the Speakers of Georgia, Moldova, and Ukraine" (RT 2018f).

However, there was zero mention of the fact its honored guest was once the unapologetic leader of a neo-Nazi movement—the Social-National Party of Ukraine. According to Britain's Channel 4, the Social-National Party was "a fascist party styled on Hitler's Nazis, with membership restricted to ethnic Ukrainians" (Whelan 2014) while Germany's *Spiegel* (2014) explained how the party's name was "an intentional reference to Adolf Hitler's National Socialist party," and that the extremist organization had an openly anti-Semitic platform. This speaks volumes about Atlantic Council's scruples when it brings someone like Parubiy—whose neo-Nazi party once boasted "we are the last hope of the white race"—to speak about "European values."

The Atlantic Council on Ukraine and Burisma

The Atlantic Council predictably blames the entire Ukrainian crisis since 2014 on Russia, presenting the conflict in Manichean terms as a struggle of good versus evil or as democracy versus authoritarianism. A key criticism is therefore the West's weak response to Russia, followed by policy recommendations that include, for example, a stronger U.S. naval presence in the Black Sea, offering Ukraine NATO membership, and pumping more weapons into Ukraine (Dickson 2018; Blank 2020; Goncharenko 2020; Reznikov 2020). Russia's media presence in the West is deemed problematic and must be confronted with more funding for counter-propaganda (Forsyth 2016; Vrabel, Janda, and Vichova 2016; Poliakova 2017). It does not seem unreasonable to assume that the Atlantic Council expects some of the "counter-propaganda" funds to be directed their way.

Awkward moments occur when journalists report on the corrupt ties of the Atlantic Council by mistake, as they are themselves convinced about the virtuous posturing of the think tank. For instance, here is a September 2019 tweet from Max Seddon, a reporter at the Moscow office of the *Financial Times*: "One curious fact about Mykola Zlochevksy, whose Ukrainian gas company Burisma employed Hunter Biden—he sponsors @AtlanticCouncil, known for its stance vs Ukrainian corruption. Here his daughter is with @anders_aslund and @JohnEdHerbst just last week."

Anders Aslund and John Herbst, who were both referenced in the comment, had the previous week held a meeting with Ukrainian companies to push market-driven "reforms." Aslund also serves on the board of the Ukrainian bank Credit Dnepr, which is owned by oligarch Pinchuk—who helps bankroll the Atlantic Council.

What makes Seddon's tweet amusing is how he presents the Atlantic Council as fighting against corruption in Ukraine while taking substantial funds from Ukrainian oligarchs: characters who hardly made their money from running corner shops. Plus, the fact Burisma employed Hunter Biden, who played a starring role in the big U.S. political scandal of autumn 2019, hardly speaks of a commitment to moral purity. Then again, the media today is so beholden to the think tank racket that such contradictions are not hugely surprising.

Burisma's hiring of Hunter Biden was part of a wider campaign by the company to improve its image in the West and to gain favors from Washington when Kiev became an American ally after the 2014 Maidan. Three months after the Western-backed coup in Ukraine in February 2014, Hunter Biden and a close family friend of U.S. Secretary of State, John Kerry, became board members of the Ukrainian gas and oil company Burisma (Sonne and Grimaldi 2014). The job paid $50.000 a month despite Hunter Biden having no experience or competencies in either the gas industry or Ukraine. When Burisma and its board members, including Hunter Biden, were under investigation for corruption by the Ukrainian Prosecutor General Viktor Shokin, Joe Biden intervened by having him fired through threats of withholding a $1 billion U.S. loan guarantee. Vice President Joe Biden insisted that the decision was not related to Burisma or his son, claiming that he has "never spoken to my son about his overseas business dealing" (Morris and Fonrouge 2020). However, the infamous emails from Hunter Biden's laptop confirmed that Joe Biden was deeply involved in providing the new job for his son (Morris and Fonrouge 2020).

As *The Wall Street Journal* revealed, in November 2019, Burisma also hired Blue Star, a consulting group founded by top officials in the

Clinton administration that specialized in preparing former Soviet-bloc countries to join NATO. They were the ones who pursued connections with lobbyists and members of the think tank racket. And here is a key line: "Burisma later became a sponsor of a Washington think tank, the Atlantic Council, whose experts are often cited on energy and security policy in the former Soviet Union." This is presumably related to the fact that "Mr Zlochevsky's campaign to burnish Burisma's image typified a common strategy among the newly rich tycoons of the former Soviet Union, who sought to keep their grip on properties they had acquired under questionable circumstances."

Thomas Grove and Alan Cullison outlined how Burisma and Atlantic Council got into bed together. "Blue Star also approached the Atlantic Council in 2016 as a possible donor. Fred Kempe, president and chief executive of the council, said the think tank rejected the overture because of Burisma's outstanding criminal cases in Ukraine" (Grove and Cullison 2019). However, as *The Wall Street Journal* reported: "Burisma hired well-connected operatives in Washington to help persuade Ukrainian prosecutors to drop criminal cases against it" (Grove and Cullison 2019). After the criminal cases were dropped, the marriage between Burisma and the Atlantic Council could proceed:

> The Atlantic Council revisited the issue, he said, when Burisma reported that the cases were dismissed. They signed a three-year contract under which Burisma has donated $100,000 a year to the think tank's Eurasia Center, whose declared mission is to defend Ukraine's national sovereignty and advocate for economic and political change, including combating corruption.

"We did our own internal due diligence, and were satisfied that we could add them to our roster of supporters," said Mr. Kempe, who noted that Burisma is one of 17 donors to the center. In January 2017, Burisma announced that it would be funding a new program with the Atlantic Council on European and international energy security, which it called "a new chapter of cooperation with the United States and

Europe together with such a high-profile organization as the Atlantic Council."

Another American reporter, Max Blumenthal, noted how the U.S. establishment press ignored the Atlantic Council's relationship with Burisma during the Trump-Joe Biden battle, which focussed on the dealings of the latter's son, Hunter, in Ukraine: "[it wasn't] overlooked because the Atlantic Council is a bit player, but because of its success in leveraging millions from foreign governments, the arms and energy industries, and Western-friendly oligarchs to bring its influence to bear in the nation's capital," he argues. "The Atlantic Council functions as the semi-official think tank of NATO in Washington. As such, it cultivates relationships with well-established policymakers who take a hard line against Russia and support the treaty organization's perpetual expansion."

Blumenthal feels the Burisma connection has not been overlooked by U.S. mainstream media but has been deliberately ignored. He points out that "A year before the Atlantic Council initiated its partnership with Burisma, the think tank had published a paper describing Zlochevsky as "openly on the take" and deriding board members Hunter Biden and former Polish President Aleksander Kwasniewski as his "trophy foreigners (Kwasniewski is today a member of the Atlantic Council's international advisory board)."

Blumenthal has also researched how the Atlantic Council has broadened its financial base by acting as a lobby for its donors:

> In 2015, for instance, the think tank helped prepare a proposal for arming the Ukrainian military with offensive weaponry like Javelin anti-tank missiles. Given that the Atlantic Council has been funded by the two manufacturers of the Javelin system, Raytheon and Lockheed Martin, this created at least the appearance of a conflict of interest. In fact, the think tank presented its Distinguished Business Leadership Award to Lockheed CEO Marillyn Hewson that same year.

Dubious arrangements like these are not limited to arms manufacturers. Anders Aslund, a neoliberal economist who helps oversee the Atlantic Council's programming on Russia and Eastern Europe, was quietly paid by a consortium of Latvian banks to write an October 2017 paper highlighting the supposed progress they had made in battling corruption. Aslund was asked to write the piece by Sally Painter, a longtime lobbyist for Latvian financial institutions who was appointed to the Atlantic Council board in 2017. At the time, one of those banks was seeking access to the U.S. market and facing allegations that it had engaged in money laundering.

Pay-for-play collaborations have helped the Atlantic Council's annual revenue grow from $2 million to over $21 million in the past decade (*New York Times* 2016). *The New York Times* even printed excerpts from the pamphlets of the Atlantic Council, which advertised "priority access to global decision makers" for corporations that donate money to the think tank. In almost every case, the think tank has churned out policy prescriptions that seem suited to its donors' interests." The corruption of the U.S. political system as a source of distortion was hiding in plain sight through the Atlantic Council.

6. PNAC: The Neoconservative Think Tank

The Project for a New American Century (PNAC) was created in 1997 to promote a security strategy based on U.S. global dominance in the new century. Founding members included Paul Wolfowitz, Donald Rumsfeld, Francis Fukuyama, and others. PNAC Directors William Kristol and Robert Kagan argued that the end of the Cold War should not fundamentally change U.S. foreign policy:

> Today, the absence of a Soviet empire does not alter the fundamental purposes of American foreign policy. … American statesmen today ought to recognize that their charge is not to await the arrival of the next great threat, but rather to shape the international environment to prevent such a threat from arising in the first place. (Kagan and Kristol 2000).

Perpetuating global dominance requires the U.S. to weaken rising powers. In 1996, Kristol and Kagan had argued in *Foreign Affairs* that in response to China's rise the U.S. had to "devise an overall strategy for containing, influencing, and ultimately seeking to change the regime in Beijing." As Russia began to recover in the 2000s, a similar sentiment was promoted toward dealing with Russia.

PNAC is most renowned for its intimate ties to the Bush administration. Paul Wolfowitz, Donald Rumsfeld, Dick Cheney, Richard Armitage, and other neoconservative hawks from PNAC obtained key positions in the Bush White House. Much like the think tanks of the Democratic Party, such as CNAS, it was also the policy recommendation of PNAC that the U.S. acquire the military capability to fight several major wars simultaneously. Most importantly, PNAC was a strong advocate for invading Iraq. Besides pushing George Bush to go to war against Iraq, PNAC also had a central role in selling the war to the public. Media engagement and policy papers were churned out. Think tanks such as AEI and the Brookings Institution also assisted.

7. CNAS: A Revolving Door for the Military Industrial Complex

The Center for a New American Security (CNAS) has been referred to as "the Military-Industrial-Think Tank Complex" as it was the largest recipient of funding from defense contractors between 2014 and 2019 (Heinz and Jung 2021). Besides the lucrative military industry, CNAS also receives huge sums from big business—oil companies like Chevron and BP, financial giants such as Bank of America and JP Morgan Chase, and Amazon and Google from Big Tech. Does the weapon industry and energy industry expect a return on their investments in CNAS? The former CEO of CNAS is none other than Victoria Nuland, a key architect behind the 2014 coup in Ukraine and U.S. policy there, going foward.

CNAS was founded by Michèle Flournoy and Kurt Campbell, who both served in the Pentagon and see military solutions to all problems. Flournoy acknowledged that the corporate giants financing think tanks expect something in return: "Every funder has intent. They're giving you money for a reason. And what you have to ensure in running a think tank is that that bias does not creep into your analysis or constrain your analysis" (Heiz 2021). Flournoy does not merely speculate about what the defense contractors want in return for its investments, as Flournoy is a board member of defense contractor Booz Allen Hamilton. Her hawkish credentials and thus value to Pentagon contractors were established early on as she drafted the 1997 Quadrennial Defense Review, which reasoned that the U.S. had to be "capable of fighting and winning two major theater wars nearly simultaneously." Thereafter she developed a counterinsurgency policy for Afghanistan, and contributed to convincing Obama to invade Libya in 2011 (Findijs 2022).

Although its business model entails giving CNAS's financial sponsors a role in determining its research focus, there is not sufficient disclosure about the link between the financial contributions and the "research output." Simply put, CNAS is an important facilitator of the U.S. corporate state, in which powerful industries can advance their profits by influencing security policy and foreign policy. Against such an array, democratic opposition does not stand a chance. Despite the U.S. public becoming increasingly apprehensive about war, CNAS policy recommendations predictably entail support for the never-ending wars, ramping up pressure on Russia and bringing China to heel.

Incubating Politicians Awaiting a Return to Government

CNAS does not only produce "experts" and "research reports" that conveniently advance the commercial interests of its investors. A key source of influence attractive to its investors is that CNAS has politicians on its payroll. The "revolving door project," an initiative to promote greater transparency about the activities of think tanks, demonstrates how CNAS has become renowned for being a waiting room for officials out of office, before sending them back into politics on a mission from the military-industrial complex. CNAS functions an incubator from which presidential administrations select foreign policy personnel.

The original objective of CNAS appeared to be to usher Hillary Clinton into the presidency. When CNAS was established, *The New York Times* noted the following:

> A coterie of national security and defense experts from the last Clinton administration have formed a new Washington think tank, the Center for a New American Security, that looks an awful lot like a shadow policy apparatus for Hillary Rodham Clinton's presidential campaign. (Healy 2007).

Leaving no doubt about the unsavory connections between politicians and think tanks, Hillary Clinton also gave the inauguration speech for CNAS. The election loss of Clinton to Obama in 2008 was not the end of this military-industrial think-tank complex masquerading as an academic institution. Instead, CNAS was able to link itself to Obama and CNAS people obtained key roles in his administration. Case in point: Michèle Flournoy, the cofounder of CNAS, became the Undersecretary of Defense for Policy. Susan Rice, a CNAS board member, became Obama's UN ambassador. CNAS has also been attributed with the achievement of influencing Obama to walk back his election promises of ending the Iraq War. *The New Yorker* reported:

> Last month, the Center for a New American Security, which has become something like Obama's foreign-policy think tank, released a report that argued against a timetable for withdrawal, regardless of the state of the war, and in favor of "conditional engagement," declaring, "Under this strategy, the United States would not withdraw its forces based on a firm unilateral schedule. Rather, the time horizon for redeployment would be negotiated with the Iraqi government and nested within a more assertive approach to regional diplomacy. (Packer 2008).

The great message of hope and change that invigorated and mobilized the American public to elect Obama was successfully reversed. The presidential candidate who ran on a peace platform became another war president and the king of drone strikes. Bush, his predecessor, was similarly elected to end Clinton's nation-building, but then, at the advice of PNAC, had started even greater nation-building projects in Afghanistan and Iraq. Think tanks have played a clear role in reversing the peace mandate of presidents. So much for democratic elections influencing policy.

In 2020, CNAS demonstrated yet again the extent of its influence over U.S. foreign policy by "buying" a presidential administration. Under the new U.S. presidential administration, at least 16 CNAS alumni have been selected for foreign policy positions. (Heinz and Jung 2021). Flourney, the cofounder of CNAS, was herself close to becoming the Secretary of Defense under the Biden administration. However, this position, intended for a civilian, was instead filled by General Lloyd Austin, who was also a board member at Raytheon—one of the world's largest weapon manufacturers. CNAS was also pushing heavily for making Kamala Harris the vice president as Harris's foreign policy advisory team consists of an army of CNAS think tankers—including Flournoy.

The Business of War

How does CNAS influence policies toward Russia? Are there efforts to explore how the failure of establishing a mutually acceptable post-Cold settlement has fuelled mutual distrust? Are there any initiatives to mitigate the security dilemma through mutual disarmament? No. Citing specific examples of CNAS policy recommendations is somewhat pointless as the conclusion is always that Russia is a threat that must be confronted head-on.

However, Russia must compete with China for the belligerent attention of CNAS. With funding from both the defense industry and Taiwan, CNAS developed war games in which it simulated a war with China. CNAS's shameless war propaganda and efforts to whip up anti-China sentiments among the public were even aired on NBC's Meet the Press. Flournoy (2020) had written an article in *Foreign Affairs* in 2020 calling for restoring military supremacy in East Asia to ensure peace and stability. When the defense industry is paying your bills it is simply bad for business to suggest disarmament and trust-building. Instead, Flournoy argued that in order "to prevent a war in Asia" it was necessary for the U.S. to develop "the capability to credibly threaten to sink all of China's military vessels, submarines, and merchant ships in the South China Sea within 72 hours."

In October 2022, CNAS fellows appeared on Australian TV to discuss how Australia could be used to contain Chinese influence. One of the CNAS think tankers, Becca Wasser who also works on "wargaming" for RAND, discussed the need to place the U.S. nuclear-capable

B-52 in Australia as a message to China: "Having bombers that could range and potentially attack mainland China could be very important in sending a signal to China that any of its actions over Taiwan could also expand further," (Findijs 2022).

8. RAND Corporation: Think tank of the intelligence agencies

The name RAND is an acronym for research and development. The think tank was founded in 1948 by Douglas Aircraft Company in an effort to involve private organizations in military planning. The U.S. was demobilizing after the conclusion of the Second World War and RAND sought to preserve the skillset and industries for future challenges. RAND includes research in political science, sociology, psychology, and communication theory, and positions its research as being practical and policy-oriented.

RAND has been based on a public/private agreement and is funded primarily by the arms manufacturers and the U.S. government. RAND is possibly the best case study on the interdependent relationship between think tanks, the intelligence agencies and the military, as RAND has since its establishment had a role in planning U.S. coups and wars.

Stanley Kubrick's movie "Dr. Strangelove or How I Learned to Stop Worrying and Love the Bomb" is a satire based on the RAND Corporation (Abella 2009: 2), addressing how nuclear war planning went off the rails during the Cold War. At that time, the military planners were measuring everything in relative power to the extent they were willing to sustain American losses in the tens of millions as long as they would inflict higher losses on the Soviets. In other words, the military's goal of winning wars is prioritized above the objective of preserving peace, irrespective of loss of American lives.

Daniel Ellsberg, a RAND analyst who later leaked the Pentagon Papers during the Vietnam War, argued that the movie resembled a documentary rather than a satire (Kaplan 2004).

Extending Russia: Competing from Advantageous Ground

RAND has produced thousands of reports, although the 326-page long report that best outlines the U.S. strategy towards Russia is the 2019 report, "Extending Russia: Competing from Advanageous Ground." The report presents the objective of defeating Russia, foregoing discussion of a defensive and passive containment of Russia to sustain peace. For RAND, the goal is to provoke and destabilize Russia to bleed the country of its resources: "causing Russia to over-extend itself militarily or economically or causing the regime to lose domestic and/or international prestige and influence" (RAND 2019a: iii).

The authors of the report have convinced themselves that the U.S. will be able to maintain full escalation control and avoid unforeseen consequences. Through precision, RAND believes that calculated threats and provocations against Russian most sensitive security issues can force Russia into responding in a manner that deprives Russia of its strengths and exacerbates its weakness. These hawkish policy recommendations are worth examining in detail as they correspond with U.S. policy.

Arming Ukraine

RAND advocates threatening NATO expansion and arming Ukraine to increase tensions along the Donbas frontline and provoke a Russian response. It asserted that pumping weapons into Ukraine would drain Russian resources and that Moscow would pay an even greater cost if it could be provoked into intervening: "The Ukrainian military already is bleeding Russia in the Donbas region (and vice versa). Providing more U.S. military equipment and advice could lead Russia to increase its direct involvement in the conflict and the price it pays for it" (RAND 2019a: xv). In 2019, two years prior to Russia's "unprovoked" Special Military Operation, RAND had envisioned dragging Russia deeper into a Ukrainian quagmire as "an additional Russian troop presence would likely be required, leading to larger expenditures, equipment losses, and Russian casualties. The latter could become quite controversial at home, as it did when the Soviets invaded Afghanistan" (RAND 2019a: 99). However, the report warned against a full-blown war as this would enable Russia to seize territories and thus possibly result in strategic victories for Moscow. Instead, low-intensity conflict to bleed Russia was the way to go.

When Russia invaded three years later, the ominous objective of bleeding Russia by fighting to the last Ukrainian became apparent among the U.S. leadership. Ukrainian media reports that Boris Johnson, with the likely support of the U.S., flew to Kiev when Russia and Ukraine appeared to be close to ending the war with a political settlement in March / April—to put an end to the political settlement. Johnson told Zelensky that the collective West would not sign any agreements with Russia to support an end to the war, but that the West would provide Ukraine with all the weapons it needed to continue fighting. According to Ukrainian sources, Johnson said that Russian weakness had convinced the West that a peaceful settlement should be avoided as "there is a chance to press him [Putin]. And the West wants to use it" (Stanley 2022). In other words, the West's program to bleed Russia was to be accomplished using Ukrainian troops.

U.S. Secretary of Defense Lloyd Austin also outlined the U.S. objective of weakening its adversary:

> We want to see Russia weakened to the degree that it can't do the kinds of things that it has done in invading Ukraine. ... So it [Russia] has already lost a lot of military capability. And a lot of its troops, quite frankly. And we want to see them not have the capability to very quickly reproduce that capability. (Carbonaro 2022).

That point was also made perfectly clear by Congressman Dan Crenshaw, who argued that "investing in the destruction of our adversary's military, without losing a single American troop, strikes me as a good idea." Republican Senator Lindsey Graham similarly argued that the U.S. was in a favourable position as it could fight Russia to the last Ukrainian: "I like the structural path we're on here. As long as we help Ukraine with the weapons they need and the economic support, they will fight to the last person" (Maté 2022a). The Republican leader, Mitch McConnell, was similarly frank in expressing the reality of U.S. objectives in the proxy war:

> President Zelenskyy is an inspiring leader. But the most basic reasons for continuing to help Ukraine degrade and defeat the Russian invaders are cold, hard, practical American interests. Helping equip our friends in Eastern Europe to win this war is also a direct investment in reducing Vladimir Putin's future capabilities to menace America, threaten our allies, and contest our core interests. . . . Finally, we all know that Ukraine's fight to retake its territory is neither the beginning nor end of the West's broader strategic competition with Putin's Russia. (McConnell 2022).

Retired U.S. General Keith Kellogg, a co-Chair of the think tank Center for American Security at the America First Policy Institute, similarly advocated for the proxy war against Russia with the same logic. General Kellogg argued in March 2023 that using Ukrainians to fight Russia was the "acme of professionalism" as it "takes a strategic adversary off the table" without "using any U.S. troops." And then "we can focus" on "our primary adversary, which is China."

RAND Corporation also advocated using the threat of NATO expansion in 2019 to both embolden Ukraine and pressure Russia into responding in a manner that would enable the U.S. to further "bleed" Russia: "While NATO's requirement for unanimity makes it unlikely that Ukraine could gain membership in the foreseeable future, Washington's pushing this possibility could boost Ukrainian resolve while leading Russia to redouble its efforts to forestall such a development" RAND 2019a: 99). At a Munk debate following

Russia's invasion in February 2022, Stephen Walt asked former U.S. ambassador to Moscow, Michael McFaul, why Washington continued to threaten NATO expansion even though the Europeans would not consent to the inclusion of Ukraine. When McFaul confirmed the provocation was a deliberate lie, Walt asked directly: "Did you believe that?" then added, "So, our diplomats are lying?," to which McFaul responded, "Yes. Yes, that's the real world, guys, come on."

The U.S. government, think tanks, and media were insisting that Russia's military actions had nothing to do with NATO and that Putin was not interested in any settlement. However, this was merely war propaganda to undermine any political settlement and keep the war going. Fiona Hill from the Brookings Institute confirmed in *Foreign Affairs* in September 2022 that the war was about NATO expansion and that Putin had been prepared to make a deal:

> According to multiple former senior U.S. officials we spoke with, in April 2022, Russian and Ukrainian negotiators appeared to have tentatively agreed on the outlines of a negotiated interim settlement: Russia would withdraw to its position on February 23, when it controlled part of the Donbas region and all of Crimea, and in exchange, Ukraine would promise not to seek NATO membership and instead receive security guarantees from a number of countries. (Hill and Stent 2022).

The U.S. also followed RAND's advice on arming and training the Ukrainian military to make it a de-facto NATO member even if de jure were out of the question. While President Obama had expressed apprehension about sending weapons to Ukraine as it could start a war, the actual U.S. policy was deliberately moving in that direction. On 10 November 2021, the U.S. and Ukraine signed the "U.S.-Ukraine Charter on Strategic Partnership" which committed Washington to develop the Ukrainian army to deepen cooperation in the Black Sea and restore Ukrainian sovereignty over Crimea. U.S. Brigadier General Joseph E. Hilbert acknowledged that the U.S. had trained more than

23,000 Ukrainian soldiers and admitted in May 2022: "the worst thing the Russians did was give us eight years to prepare" (Norman 2022).

In the first week of the Russian invasion in February 2022, Hillary Clinton argued on MSNBC that the U.S. should treat Ukraine as another Afghanistan: "I think that [Afghanistan] is the model that people are now looking toward" (MSNBC 2022). Leon Panetta, the White House chief of staff under Bill Clinton and the U.S. Secretary of Defence and CIA director under Barack Obama, had already argued in March 2022: "We are engaged in a conflict here, it's a proxy war with Russia, whether we say so or not. . . . The way you get leverage is by, frankly, going in and killing Russians" (Panetta 2022). Cas Freeman, the former U.S. Assistant Secretary of Defense for International Security Affairs and Director for Chinese Affairs at the U.S. State Department, argued that the U.S. is fighting a proxy war against Russia in Ukraine. According to Freeman, the sentiment in Washington is that "we will fight to the last Ukrainian," which implies policies are aimed to prolong rather than end the war. He stated that:

> the United States is not part of any effort to negotiate an end to the fighting. To the extent that there is mediation going on, it seems to be by Turkey, possibly Israel, maybe China. That's about it. And the United States is not in the room. Everything we are doing, rather than accelerating an end to the fighting and some compromise, seems to be aimed at prolonging the fighting, assisting the Ukrainian resistance—which is a noble cause, I suppose, but that will result in a lot of dead Ukrainians as well as dead Russians" (Maté 2022b).

RAND's fear in 2019 that the proxy war could lead to unpredictability or a strategic victory for Russia began to materialize in early 2023. RAND subsequently released a new report in January 2023 with the title: "Avoiding a Long War U.S. Policy and the Trajectory of the Russia-Ukraine Conflict." While the report recognized the benefit of continuing to weaken Russia, it now appeared to realize that the negative consequences of a long war were outweighing the benefits. The risks of a direct NATO-Russia war and the use of nuclear weapons were at the top of U.S. security concerns. While extending Russia by bleeding it slowly is beneficial, the loss of strategic territory in Ukraine undermines the objective of competing from advantageous ground. More on this in the last chapter.

Fuelling the Civil War in Syria

RAND noted in 2019 that the Syrian war was settling and possibly coming to an end. However, this could be reversed as increased military support to the opposition fighters "could perpetuate and intensify a civil war that had begun to wind down, thereby imposing attritional costs on both Russia and Iran" (RAND 2019a: 106).

Previous policy recommendations from RAND, dating back to 2008, had outlined strategies to fuel divisions and civil war within Syria through "covert action, information operations, unconventional warfare" consistent with a "divide and rule" strategy. RAND argued that the U.S. should "capitalize on the 'Sustained Shia-Sunni Conflict' trajectory by taking the side of the conservative Sunni regimes against [Iran-allied Shiite empowerment movements in the Muslim world" (RAND 2008: xvi). The report also recommended controlling oil supplies in Syria: "The geographic area of proven oil reserves coincides with the power base of much of the Salafi-jihadist network. This creates a linkage between oil supplies and the long war that is not easily broken or simply characterized" (RAND 2008: 171).

Another think tank, the Center for Strategic and International Studies (CSIS), organized a talk with the Syria Study Group in 2019, in which the Democratic co-chair argued the U.S. military "owned" one-third of Syrian territory that is resource-rich in terms of hosting its hydrocarbons and agriculture. Controlling the resources would enable the U.S. to prevent reconstruction as government-controlled territory would remain a "rubble," and control over these resources would also give the U.S. influence in any future Syrian settlement (CSIS 2019).

Promoting Regime Change in Belarus

Belarus was also identified as a key target as a significant Russian ally. RAND advocated the promotion of regime change as "Successfully promoting regime change and altering the country's orientation westward would be a real blow to Moscow." Regime change could also be instrumental in breaking up the Eurasian Economic Union: "it would undermine Russia's attempt to create an EEU in competition with the EU" (RAND 2019a). This advice was consistent with former statements by U.S. Secretary of State, Hillary Clinton, who had argued in 2012 that the U.S. was seeking to sabotage the Eurasian Economic Union: "we are trying to figure out effective ways to slow down or prevent it" (Clover 2012). Even if U.S. regime change efforts were not successful, the instability would drain Russian resources: "From a U.S. policy standpoint, Belarus' unrest might present an opportunity to extend Russia by aiding the opposition" The report goes on to argue that Russia would be burdened with supporting a Belarussian dependency, which could also fuel local resistance. One year following the RAND report, the U.S. and its allies were fuelling protests in Belarus in 2020 with overt demands for regime change. (Rand 2019a)

Exploit Tensions in the South Caucasus

RAND recognizes the opportunities to "exploit tensions in the South Caucasus." Two different strategies were recommended to overextend and weaken Russia: "the United States could push for a closer NATO relationship with Georgia and Azerbaijan, likely leading Russia to strengthen its military presence in South Ossetia, Abkhazia, Armenia, and southern Russia," or "Alternatively, the United States could try to induce Armenia to break with Russia" (RAND 2019a: 117).

Russia's position as the leading security provider in the South Caucasus largely relies on maintaining a good relationship with two key adversaries—Armenia and Azerbaijan. Reigniting conflict between these two states would place Russia in a dilemma as support for Armenia would alienate Azerbaijan, while the failure to support Armenia would undermine the security commitments to a member of the Russian-led Collective Security Treaty Organisation (CSTO). One year following the RAND report, Azerbaijan went to war to take control over the disputed territories in Armenian-controlled Nagorno-Karabakh.

Reducing Russian Influence in Central Asia and Moldova

RAND recognizes that Russia has benefitted from economic cooperation and integration with Eurasian powers, particularly from the Chinese Belt and Road Initiative and the Eurasian Economic Union, contending that the objective for the U.S. should therefore be "to reduce Russia's benefits from both of these" economic projects. It is argued that the U.S. could increase trade with Central Asia to reduce their relative trade with Russia, although the disadvantage is that the economic growth of Central Asia would lead to absolute trade with Russia increasing (RAND 2019a).

Policy recommendations are also outlined for diminishing Russian influence in Moldova. The main instrument of power is evidently to promote EU and NATO expansion, although RAND also mulls the possibility of integrating Moldova into Romania. Other policy options include convincing Moldova to terminate the 1994 peace agreement to force out Russian peacekeepers from Transnistria.

Escalating Military Tensions Across All Domains

RAND recommended that "the United States can exploit Russia's anxieties about its vulnerability in the air and space domains." Russia can be pressured to spend more on its military if the U.S. begins "modernizing the air and missile components of the nuclear triad," or alternatively "Deploying bombers to distant bases around Russia's periphery would certainly get Moscow's attention and raise Russian anxieties" (RAND 2019a).

Washington also followed recommendations from RAND on nuclear weapons, which included:

> U.S. leaders could probably goad Russia into a costly arms race by breaking out of the nuclear arms control regime. Washington could abrogate New START and begin aggressively adding to its nuclear stockpile and to its air and missile delivery systems. Moscow would almost certainly follow suit, whatever the cost" (RAND 2019a).

RAND points out that in maritime warfare, the U.S. also enjoys a strategic advantage. Much of Russian history has been about securing reliable access to the sea, as Spykman (1942: 182) recognized: "since the time of Peter the Great, Russia has attempted to break through the encircling ring of border states and the reach the ocean. Geography and sea power have persistently thwarted her." Thus, British and U.S. containment strategies have to a great extent been focused on denying Russia maritime access. After the Cold War, NATO expansion and other U.S. policies have pushed back Russian access to the Black Sea, the Baltic Sea, and the Arctic.

RAND recommends that the U.S. exploit these Russian fears with a more hostile military posture along Russia's maritime borders:

> More-aggressive U.S. and allied patrolling near Russian naval base areas could cause Russia to adopt expensive countermeasures. With limited access to the open sea, Russia would be sensitive to threats posed to these areas—particularly the Arctic, home of its nuclear ballistic missile submarine fleet, and the Baltic and Black Seas. (RAND 2019a: xvii).

This policy could be advanced through Greater NATO cooperation with Sweden and Finland in the Baltic Sea to create security threats against the Russian navy. RAND recognizes that threatening Russia's nuclear-powered ballistic missile submarines would pressure Russia to invest in expensive counter-measures, although it carries with it the risk of "a first strike from Russia" (RAND 2019a: 201).

These policy recommendations have also seemingly been followed. The efforts to expand NATO into Ukraine were consistent with a longer strategy of seizing control over the Black Sea. NATO's Deputy Secretary-General argued in July 2022 that most of the war in Ukraine is about control over the Black Sea (Euronews 2022). With the expansion of NATO into Sweden and Finland, the former NATO Secretary-General Anders Fogh Rasmussen opined that Russian access to the Baltic Sea can be suspended: "after the accession of Finland and Sweden to NATO, the Baltic Sea will now be a NATO sea . . . if we wish, we can block all entry and exit to Russia through St. Petersburg" (Lrt 2022).

Ideological and Informational Measures

In 2019, RAND advocated for intensifying the ideological and information war against Russia to weaken the legitimacy and stability of the Russian government. It is argued that "Western policymakers seeking to deter or discredit Russia would appear to have found fertile ground in the regime's sensitivity to domestic unrest and foreign ostracism." Under the heading "pathways for influence operations," the report cites "election upsets, mass protests, and civil disobedience" as means of delegitimizing the government (RAND 2019a: 138–39).

Navalny is named as a credible authority due to his anti-corruption work and activism, which can be used to destabilize the government. The report goes on to argue, "if damaging information could be acquired" against Russian authorities, then it could be "leaked through an intermediary" with continuing references to Navalny as a credible source. Yet, RAND cautions that plausible deniability is imperative: "it would seem highly inadvisable for Western intelligence agencies to attempt to cooperate directly with anticorruption groups inside Russia, such as Navalny's Anti-Corruption Foundation. Such cooperation would undermine the effectiveness of those groups within Russia" (RAND 2019a: 163).

9. CEPA: Mobilising Central and Eastern Europe against Russia

The Warsaw and Washington–based Centre for European Policy Analysis (CEPA) claims to be "the leading research institute dedicated to the study of Central-East Europe and Russia." This description sounds impressive and high-minded, but at this point, we have learned not to take think tanks at face value, so let us see who is bankrolling it. Despite CEPA's insistence that it is a "public policy research institute" attempting to "promote an economically vibrant, strategically secure, and politically free Europe with close and enduring ties to the United States," the reality is that the group is primarily dedicated to military issues.

CEPA amounts to a home for media figures who devote their careers to opposing Russia. It whips up tensions, even when they do not really exist, presumably in order to drum up business for its sponsors, who are heavily drawn from the military industry. For example, it spent much of 2017 hyping up the "threat" from Russia and Belarus's joint Zapad exercises, even running a sinister-looking countdown clock before the long-planned training commenced. CEPA grossly overestimated the size of the event, saying it "could be the largest military exercise since the end of the Cold War" and dismissing basically all Moscow's statements on its actual nature as "disinformation."

Sometimes CEPA crosses the border into the ridiculous. For instance, it alleged before the 2018 World Cup that "the Russians" may drug England's soccer team to prevent them from performing well at the event. This was carried on BBC and in the *Daily Mail*, based on the "expertise" of a Senior Fellow at the Center for European Policy Analysis (CEPA).

At times the thin line between the lobbyists and think tank fellows disappears completely. Kurt Volker is a Distinguished Fellow at CEPA fellow who was a former U.S. Ambassador to NATO and former U.S. Special Representative for Ukraine Negotiations from 2017 to 2019. But also: Volker is an advisor for BGR Government Affairs (BGR), a lobbying and communications firm, which lobbies on behalf of Pentagon contractors to sell weapons.

Kurt Volker took a strong position against peace when Russia sought security guarantees from NATO in 2021. In June 2021, President Joe Biden and President Vladimir Putin met in Geneva in an effort to improve relations and restore what Biden referred to as "a predictable and rational relationship." However, Volker opposed peace and reconciliation with Russia. He wrote that the route to "success is confrontation" as any accommodation of Russia was tantamount to appeasement:

> [A]ny outcome that seems reassuring and benign on the surface actually works in Putin's favor. For the U.S., therefore, the best possible outcome is not one of modest agreements and a commitment to "predictability," but one of a lack of agreements altogether. Success is confrontation" (Volker 2021).

In February 2022, only days before Russia invaded after failing to obtain security guarantees from NATO, Volker (2022) published an article in CEPA arguing: "the United States and NATO allies need to get far more serious about helping Ukraine defend itself. . . . We have been through this before. It will be difficult, but we must pull ourselves together to defeat this kind of aggression." The article failed to disclose Volker's affiliation to BGR.

While other think tanks at least try to make their funding look semi-organic, CEPA appears to have zero hang-ups about its role as a mouthpiece for defense contractors. Which is, at least, honest. FireEye, Lockheed Martin, Raytheon, Bell Helicopters, and BAE systems pump funds into it, and they are joined by the U.S. State Department and the Department of Defense and other American government cutouts. Another notable paymaster is the National Endowment for Democracy's regime change experts, who are surely interested in CEPA's remit to also cover Belarus. Accordingly, there is the usual money not just from the National Endowment for Democracy, but also from NATO. But what makes CEPA "special" is the share of arms manufacturers on its contributor list, which is far greater than comparable outfits.

At this point you might be asking: why are weapons dealers so interested in bankrolling a faux-academic lobby firm in Poland? Well, this has its origin in the NATO expansionism that began in the 1990s, which became the source of billions of dollars in weapon contracts. It is obvious CEPA is a logical progression of that sort of policy, as it extends its activities into Eastern Europe itself, whipping up hysteria about "Russia threats" and thus "encouraging" policymakers to bump up military spending.

In late August 2019, CEPA's online home page was exclusively focused on Russia and the Baltics, with no mention of any European states west of Kaliningrad. Meanwhile, its featured sections included "Europe's Edge" (focused on countries bordering Russia, which obviously is not considered to be "European," by the think tank) and Power Vertical (described as "Kremlin coverage for Kremlin watchers").

That said, its most interesting focus was on the "Road To Union Shield," which was a relatively innocuous Russian-Belarussian joint training operation. This coverage was especially notable because, back in 2017, CEPA placed a huge emphasis on another Minsk-Moscow exercise, in a series dubbed (you guessed it), The Road to Zapad 2017. And the only real difference was the presence of "the" in the title.

Back then, the lobbyists posited whether Zapad ("west" in Russian) would "be a harmless and transparent military exercise or will it (sic) act as a springboard for conflict on Europe's doorstep?" During its updates, CEPA promoted the idea that 100,000 Russian soldiers would participate in the maneuvers. This estimate was also pushed by senior NATO figures, and a large number of western media.

For instance, *The Economist* wrote, without any qualification or attribution,

> Zapad 2017 is expected to involve at least 100,000 Russian troops. It will extend across the country's Western Military District and Belarus, which has a border with three NATO members. By next week, most of the advance elements of the forces taking part in the exercise will have arrived. The rest, expected a fortnight later, will include the First Guards Tank Army, a famous unit from the second world war that was reformed in 2015. It packs a mighty offensive punch.

In the end, Zapad turned out to be something of an anti-climax for the fear factories, whom the Carnegie Endowment described as "circulating speculation and alarmist theories that became further and further divorced from the underlying facts."

Ultimately, Belarus stated about 12,700 personnel took part in Zapad 2017 on its territory. Meanwhile, Lieutenant Colonel Thomas Möller, a Swedish army observer, later told German State broadcaster, Deutsche Welle, that Stockholm had concluded even fewer were involved, only something like 12,400. Of course, for CEPA, the key was to whip up a storm of hysteria. Russia's neighbors' fear of Moscow's intentions is profitable for the bottom line of their paymasters. For proof of this, note how Poland signed a $4.75 billion dollar deal to buy Raytheon's Patriot missile system just over six months later.

Now, of course, Warsaw did not solely sign the contract because of CEPA's agitation. But it is also true that the anti-Russian frenzy drummed up by the think tank is beneficial to its interests, and clearly a helpful lobbying tool. Indeed, in the spring of 2019, Raytheon opened a new "state-of-the-art" headquarters in Warsaw, declaring it "a visible reminder that Raytheon is part of the Polish community," throwing in a few property porn lines such as "close to the U.S. embassy, it stands six stories high and enjoys a river backdrop." Because it's probably more soothing to hawk destructive weapons within view of a flowing body of water.

Of course, what also benefits CEPA's sponsors is how its faux-academic ramblings help in the information space. "These think tanks enjoy an undue air of independence. Experts who work for these defense contractor-funded institutes are quoted frequently in mainstream newspapers and invited on mainstream channels, where they are presented as independent voices," notes journalist Danielle Ryan. "But those independent voices somehow always seem to be in favor of policies that benefit weapons manufacturers." It seems the more money defense contractors throw at think tanks, the more those think tanks will argue in favor of the military policies that will make those companies the most money. It is a vicious cycle, but one which does not take much think tank-style analysis to figure out, she continues. "The sad thing for the think tank lobbyists is that the money they make calling for war is nothing in comparison to the money Lockheed, Raytheon, Boeing, and the rest make from it. Maybe they should ask for a raise."

Ryan also noted how "a glance at the Twitter feed of CEPA reveals almost obsession-like focus on the so-called threat from Russia. In 2016, the think tank suggested in a report on information warfare that people who have 'fallen victim to Kremlin propaganda' should be 'deradicalized' in special programs."

This brings us to another CEPA preoccupation: the idea that Western countries must use propaganda as a battlefield against Russia. In the summer of 2016, it hired Peter Pomerantsev, who at the time was lobbying for the pro-Brexit Legatum Institute in London, to author a paper on "Winning the Information War" with Edward Lucas, its own employee who, back then, also moonlighted as an editor at *The Economist* magazine.

In a reminder of how tiny the think tank world is, the study included contributions from Anne Applebaum and Ben Nimmo. And, as Ryan said, yes it seriously suggested members of the public "who have fallen victim to Kremlin propaganda" should be subjected to the same methods used to "deradicalize far-right extremists and jihadists."

Canadian Professor Paul Robinson had a similar opinion of the dispatch."Lucas and Pomerantsev seem to share the misperception by many politicians that it is not their policies that are wrong, it is just the way that they are communicated to the public. Clampdown on your opponent's propaganda and improve your own, and all will be well," he wrote. "This approach may be emotionally satisfying, but it ignores the deeper reasons why people choose to disbelieve you and believe somebody else."

Robinson's interpretation was that Lucas and Pomerantsev were "suggesting anti-brainwashing programs for people who watch RT." Of course, some may regard Russia's foreign broadcaster as "propaganda," but fundamentally it is a news organization offering a different spin, to varying degrees, on how traditional Western Mainstream Media covers the news, often reporting stories that are ignored, for whatever reason, by their Western competitors.

Indeed, if the establishment press in the European Union and North America adequately covered these subjects, fewer people would read or watch RT or any of the independent media which also upsets gatekeepers in the think tank racket. That said, does RT take a pro-Russian line on foreign policy? Yes, there is no doubt it does, as do the BBC and CNN take a pro-British and pro-American perspective on foreign policy. You will search long and hard before you will find a CNN or BBC staffer who thinks Russia (or China, or any other Western "enemy") is right and the U.S. and UK are wrong in any dispute. This is just how things are, for better or worse.

It's important to look at the key people at CEPA because this pressure group has more media clout than most of its peers. Again, predictably, their funding by American arms makers, NATO, and the U.S. government is never mentioned when their columns are published or their punditry is included in broadcasts.

First up, there is the grandiose-sounding "International Advisory Council" which features some very well-known names in the Atlanticist world. There's former Swedish Prime Minister Carl Bildt, *Guardian* columnist Timothy Garton Ash, and Estonia's former President Toomas Hendrik Ilves, who was raised in the U.S., and once worked for its state broadcaster, RFE/RL. Also, the late U.S. Secretary of State Madeleine Albright is listed, along with the late Zbigniew Brzezinski, the Polish-born one-time National Security Advisor to Jimmy Carter. *The Washington Post*'s Anne Applebaum is included, having moved upstairs from a position as a "Senior Adjunct Fellow." Which is a fancy way of saying she was an especially important lobbyist.

While Applebaum is now removed from the direct participation in the fray, the front line at CEPA still packs a punch. There's Brian "Power Vertical" Whitmore, who was once described as the "Lord Haw-Haw of Prague," when he worked at RFE/RL. This was because of his video blogs, where he sat in front of a wall-mounted image of Moscow's Kremlin telling his viewership how awful Russia is. Since then (August 2016) he has switched to CEPA, where he does the very same thing, except from Washington.

It is unclear at whom the content is actually aimed. If it were meant to influence Russians, you would imagine it would be broadcast in their language because fluent English speakers comprise only a tiny percentage of the Russian population. The only explanation appears therefore to be that the purpose is to influence journalists and pundits who cover Russian affairs for Western outlets.

This, as a consequence, meant U.S. state media was essentially engaged in directing propaganda at members of the mainstream and independent America press. Of course, CEPA is also partially U.S. government-funded, but that is less obvious and blatant. Whitmore is joined by Elisabeth Braw, described as "previously a journalist, most recently with the *Christian Science Monitor*" but still "a contributor to *The Wall Street Journal*, the *Financial Times*, *Foreign Affairs*, *Foreign Policy*, and *Politico*, focusing on European security." Her articles do not mention CEPA, let alone the funding.

As it happens, one article in *The Wall Street Journal* stood out: "Stop Worrying and Learn to Love the Military-Industrial Complex" (Braw 2019). That seems like an interesting viewpoint for someone attached to a "think tank" bankrolled by the Military-Industrial Complex. By all means, it could be coincidental, but it does stand out.

Another CEPA "fellow," Maria Snegovaya, seems to be a special case. What makes Snegovaya interesting is she is a native of Russia embedded in the U.S. anti-Russia think tank matrix. If the situation were reversed, she would be denounced as a "useful idiot" of the enemy. According to CEPA's biography, she has "collaborated with the Institute for the Study of War, the Brookings Institution, the Free Russia Foundation, the National Endowment for Democracy, the Eurasia Group, and Freedom House." Before joining the think tank merry-go-round, Snegovaya wrote for the *Moscow Times*, where her pieces included "Ukraine's Crisis Is Not the West's Fault" (Snegovaya 2014). This viewpoint hardly hurt her prospects with the various U.S. government-funded outfits mentioned above.

And, lastly, Edward Lucas, another former journalist, most notably at *The Economist*, now a columnist at *The Times of London*, and very proud of his work with CEPA. What's more, Lucas believes there aren't enough CEPAs and that Western states need to invest more in what he sees as an "information war." In the spring of 2020, CEPA appointed a new "president," Alina Polyakova. In yet another example of how the think tank racket is a lucrative merry-go-round, she had previously practiced anti-Russian scaremongering at the Atlantic Council. Polyakov raised eyebrows by coming to the defense of Viktor Orban's Hungary.

While Russia has always contended that the most important quality for European members of the bloc is that they are willing to subjugate themselves to Washington's control, NATO styles itself as a protector and promoter of democracy and freedom—an alliance of like-minded nations dedicated to upholding "Western values" on both sides of the Atlantic. Meanwhile, in Eastern Europe, membership has been seen as a prerequisite for inclusion in the Western "family" itself. Alas, for NATO to exist, as we know, it needs an enemy, whether real or imagined, and Russia is the chosen adversary. This has created a bizarre situation where—due to the desire to join "the West"—a number of states have signed up to the club despite having no axe to grind with Moscow.

In Russia, to be blunt, NATO is viewed as a vehicle to serve American geopolitical interests and allow Washington to extend its armed forces ever closer to Russian borders. Experts and officials in Moscow also like to point out that its other function is as a money-spinner, as it ties most European countries to the U.S. military-industrial complex.

CEPA's cynicism was particularly egregious, especially given how the likes of Madeleine Albright, Anne Applebaum, Carl Bildt, and Toomas Hendrik Ilves have spent years promoting hegemony and militarism through the thin veil of advancing "liberal democracy." Not to mention that some of its more prominent lobbyists—such as Polyakova, Lucas, and Whitmore—have built careers on attacking "growing illiberalism" in Europe. Of course, that was back when Russia was perceived to be at the vanguard of that drift. However, now that Viktor Orban's Hungary has—very deliberately—positioned itself as the leader of the "illiberal" movement, CEPA appears to have made a stunning about-face. Thus, it enlisted none other than Kurt Volker—the former White House point man on Ukraine—to defend Budapest's policies.

"Much of the criticism of Hungary and Prime Minister Viktor Orban strikes me as shallow," he wrote. Volker then launched into a passionate defense of Orban insofar as "We need allies," clearly admitting that Hungary being on "America's side" is more important than NATO's usual high-minded rhetoric. The cynicism is stunning, exposing CEPA for what it really is. CEPA's acquiescence to Budapest's agenda is clearly fuelled by the funding it takes from Hungarian government-funded bodies. It's curiously supported by the Hungarian American Coalition and the Hungary Initiatives Foundation. Both of these receive financing from the government in Budapest.

Indeed, this cash infusion even saw Réka Szemerkényi, Hungary's former ambassador to Washington—a Orbán appointee—named as executive vice-president of the pressure group. Outfits like CEPA throw shade at Russia constantly over its refusal to follow Western norms, ignoring the fact Russia was expected to Westernize without the prospect of Western integration—even as countries such as Poland and Hungary, which have been allowed to join institutions like the European Union and NATO (and get huge amounts of money to boot), are backsliding with regard to democracy but are handed free passes. That's because this is not about values; it is about geopolitics and financial gain. Hungary's political system is Hungary's own business. Indeed, much like in Russia (where the Communists are second to United Russia), Hungary's main opposition party (nationalist Jobbik) is even more anti-Western than the government (Fidesz). The hypocrisy here entirely belongs to CEPA. Indeed, it may even be a welcome bit of honesty from the U.S. foreign policy elite—which Volker clearly represents as a career member of the "swamp."

10. Brookings Institution and Russiagate

The Brookings Institution is one of the oldest American think tanks, and has subsequently had a lot of unsavory political activities that could be explored. The Brookings Institution received much attention after its president had to resign following the revelation that he had secretly been paid to lobby for Qatar (Kirkpatrick 2022). The president of the Brookings Institution was retired four-star general John R. Allen, who had previously commanded American troops in Afghanistan. Brookings' immense financing from arms manufacturers was deemed unproblematic as this is the key component of the business model that keeps Washington running.

Other fellows at the Brookings Institution include Victoria Nuland, who had a central role in toppling Ukrainian president Yanukovich in 2014 and has been deeply engaged ever since. Then there is Janet Yellen, the former head of the Federal Reserve, allegedly apolitical. However, here, we will focus on the role of the Brookings Institution in the Russiagate hoax that took place in the aftermath of the 2016 U.S. presidential election.

The accusation that Donald Trump was the Kremlin's "Manchurian candidate" or "Siberian candidate" rested primarily on the Steele Dossier, which laid the foundation for the Russiagate investigations. The Steele Dossier consisted primarily of unverified accusations, collected in a report by a former British intelligence official, MI-6 agent Christopher Steele. The Democratic Party, the media, and the intelligence agencies all used it to challenge the legitimacy of the Trump presidency.

The Steele Dossier was eventually discredited as being based on hearsay and was full of embarrassing mistakes. As the allegations in the report were proven to be fake and its credibility collapsed, even the intelligence agencies began to distance themselves from the report. Even its author, Christopher Steele, began to walk back the claims in the report once he was sued for libel, proclaiming that the report was merely intended to provide "unverified" parts of "raw intelligence" that "warranted further investigation." So how did this piece of propaganda become the main piece of evidence in the Russiagate investigations?

It was later revealed that Christopher Steele was working for the Clinton campaign. During her presidential campaign, Clinton and her team hired Fusion GPS, a private research firm, to dig up dirt on her political rival. Fusion GPS then gave Steele the contract to investigate Donald Trump and write an incendiary report. Steele testified in a British court in August 2018 that he had been hired by the Clinton campaign to "obtain information necessary. . . . to provide legal advice on the potential impact of Russian involvement on the legal validity of the outcome of the 2016 U.S. Presidential election," in order to give the DNC and the Clinton campaign a path to legally "challenge the validity of the outcome of that election" (Scarborough 2018).

While it was initially unknown to the public that Clinton was funding Steele's "research," it must be said that CIA Director John Brennan had already briefed then-President Barack Obama on 26 July 2016 about how Clinton was fabricating a Russia-Trump conspiracy theory. In Brennan's notes to Obama, he explained that Clinton used the false allegations as "a means of distracting the public from her use of a private email server" and "to vilify Donald Trump by stirring up a scandal claiming interference by the Russian security service" (Scarborough 2020).

So, what was the role of the Brookings Institution? A primary researcher and contributor to the Steele Dossier was Igor Danchenko, an employee at Brookings Institution. Danchenko worked for several years under Fiona Hill, a senior fellow at the Brookings Institution, a renowned anti-Russian hawk who assisted Danchenko to climb the career ladder and introduced him to Christopher Steele (Episkopos 2021). In November 2021, Special Council John Durham indicted Igor Danchenko on several accounts of lying to the FBI concerning investigations into the Steele Dossier.

Danchenko had become a key source of information for the Steele Dossier after he claimed to have gathered incriminating information from a phone call and meeting in New York with the Russian-American Chamber of Commerce's president at the time, Sergey Millian. However, Millian insists he has never spoken with Danchenko on the phone, in person, or by email. Millian's statement was corroborated by an FBI investigation, which concluded that there never were any phone calls and Millian never responded to any of Danchenko's emails. The alleged meeting between Danchenko and Millian was also fake, and it was proven that Danchenko was actually at the Bronx Zoo with his family when the alleged meeting was supposed to have taken place. The greatest political scandal in modern American history included several employees of the Brookings Institution, which warrants some criticism and investigation into the malign influence of think tanks per se, insofar as the Brookings Institution was not the only think tank involved in the Russiagate hoax.

The New Knowledge think tank conducted a "false flag" operation to swing the 2017 Alabama state election. The think tank impersonated Russian election interference in favor of Republican candidate Roy Moore, and then wrote a report, "The Tactics & Tropes of the Internet Research Agency," exposing the alleged Russian interference. This report was then handed over as "evidence" to *The Washington Post* and *The New York Times*, which were hungry for stories about evil Russians in the midst of the Russiagate hoax, and ran with it. However, the election interference by the think tank was eventually exposed, with an article by the *Times* admitting that New Knowledge had fabricated Russian interference. The *Times* quoted an internal report by New Knowledge: "We orchestrated an elaborate 'false flag' operation that planted the idea that the Moore campaign was amplified on social media by a Russian botnet" (Morrow 2018).

11. ISW: The Institute for the Study of War

The Institute for the Study of War (ISW) could as easily be titled "The Institute for the Promotion of War." The ISW consistently agitates for more and more American aggression. It supported the Iraq "surge" and encouraged more involvement in Afghanistan. ISW also focuses on Syria, Libya, and Iran. One of its lobbyists, Jennifer Cafarella, called for the U.S. military to take Damascus in 2018, which would have brought Washington into direct conflict with Russia and Iran. Predictably, Raytheon has opened its wallet. Meanwhile, other U.S. military contractors like General Dynamics and DynCorp are also involved.

During the war in Ukraine, the ISW became a go-to think tank for citing updates and analyses of the war. The leading media outlets all cite this think-tank as if it were a seemingly academic and independent source of analysis. Behind this facade of objectivity is a neo-conservative and hawkish organization funded generously by Pentagon contractors. The media offers no information about the ISW whenever it is cited, despite its conflict of interest as the U.S. government spends tens of billions in military aid for Ukraine to confront Russia.

The ISW is run by Kimberly Kagan and Frederick Kagan, renowned neoconservative influencers in Washington. Fredrick Kagan is the brother of Robert Kagan, who together with Bill Kristol established the Project for a New American Century (PNAC), which took on a central role in the Bush administration's decision to invade

Iraq. Robert Kagan happens to be the husband of Victoria Nuland, who was heavily involved in the U.S.-backed coup in Ukraine in 2014 and remains engaged there. As the Assistant Secretary of State for European and Eurasian Affairs, Nuland estimated in December 2013, as the riots in Kiev were unfolding, that the U.S. had invested more than $5 billion since 1991 to assist Ukraine in achieving "the future it deserves" (Mearsheimer 2014: 80). A leaked phone call between Victoria Nuland and Geoffrey Pyatt, the U.S. Ambassador to Ukraine, revealed a plot to topple the Ukrainian government. The phone call, leaked two weeks before the coup, also discussed who should be part of the new Ukrainian government after the coup (BBC 2014a).

While there are legitimate reasons for providing military aid to a country that has been invaded, failing to disclose information that reveals less altruistic motivations is problematic. When the consumers of Western media read about the war in Ukraine based on the information from the academic-sounding Institute for the Study of War, shouldn't they be informed that this information comes from the same people who actually toppled the government in Ukraine? The readers of *The New York Times* or *The Washington Post* might be interested to know that the main think tank that their newspapers are citing is run by neoconservatives that advocate for an American empire and are funded by the arms manufacturers to achieve it.

Brookings wasn't alone; other think tanks were also involved in replacing the democratically elected government in Ukraine with one handpicked by the U.S. Case in point: the Aspen Institute, which promotes itself as a think tank whose initiatives have "an impact beyond the conference room. They are designed to provoke, further and improve actions taken in the real world." Natalie Jaresko, now the Chair of the Aspen Institute, is a U.S. citizen and former State Department official and former Economic Section Chief of the U.S. Embassy in Ukraine. After the U.S.-backed coup in Ukraine in 2014, Jaresko was made the Finance Minister of Ukraine. She received Ukrainian citizenship the same day as she took the new job. In other words, she had "an impact beyond the conference room."

12. The Institute for Statecraft and the "Integrity Initiative"

The Institute for Statecraft is yet another "pro-democracy" think tank funded by government and intelligence agencies, although presenting itself as a "private" organization doing "independent" research. According to its website, the Integrity Initiative is "dedicated to revealing and combating propaganda and disinformation." While the official objective is to defend democracy, primarily from Russia, the network functions as an instrument deployed by the British government to disseminate anti-Russian propaganda. The budget plan reveals that 95 percent of the Integrity Initiative is funded by the British government, the U.S. State Department, NATO, and Facebook.

The Integrity Initiative builds what it defines as "cluster groups," which are groups of contacts consisting of trusted journalists, academics, researchers, politicians, lobbyists, think tanks, and military personnel in foreign countries. These friendly clusters are tasked with acting in conformity to establish and cement the narrative called for by the British government. It is common knowledge in the media industry that seizing the narrative early is imperative to controlling the story, and the Integrity Initiative has thus set itself the objective of "Increasing the speed of response, mobilizing the network to activism in pursuit of the 'golden minute'" (MoA 2018). As Indian spy chief Vikram Sood (2020) argues, it is imperative to be first to establish the narrative: "tell your story first, any other story thereafter will only be a reaction."

When a dispute or conflict emerges with Russia, the coordinated efforts by the cluster groups manufacture the illusion of consensus around a narrative to manipulate group psychology and herd public opinion. The Integrity Initiative recognizes the imperative of sowing a narrative to obtain legitimacy for its policies and agenda, while concurrently denigrating the argument of Russia and anyone who may be seen as being too soft on Russia. The Integrity Initiative defines its mission:

> To counter Russian disinformation and malign influence in Europe by: expanding the knowledge base; harnessing existing expertise, and establishing a network of networks of experts, opinion formers and policy makers, to educate national audiences in the threat and to help build national capacities to counter it. (MoA 2018).

For example, on 7 June 2018, the Spanish cluster of the Integrity Initiative was able to smear and disrupt the appointment of Perto Banos as the Director of the National Security Department in Spain, whom the British government considered undesirable as he was too friendly towards Russia (MoA 2018). Leaked documents from the Integrity Initiative revealed that the operation of canceling him only took a few hours: at 14:00 the "Spanish cluster leader alerts other cluster members and prepares a dossier to inform the main Spanish media. The cluster starts a campaign on Twitter," while already at 19:45 it was reported that some Spanish diplomats and two political parties had intervened by expressing their concerns and attempting to stop the appointment (Blumenthal 2018).

The operation was eventually leaked to the media, possibly because the propaganda initiative began to target one of its sponsors' domestic political opposition. In December 2018, it was reported by the *Sunday Mail* that the Integrity Initiative was targeting the leader of the UK's domestic political opposition—Jeremy Corbyn. Shadow Justice Minister Richard Burgon demanded that "the Conservative government in this country shouldn't be using public funds or the state to undermine or attack the official opposition" (Manthorpe and Martin 2018).

Whether the leaks from the UK's "Integrity Initiative" were due to hacking or an internal leak in the spring of 2019 is unknown. But either way, the Integrity Initiative's emergence in public was something extraordinary. Put simply, the pressure group united a number of prominent figures in the UK think tank racket with well-known and well-placed members of the British mainstream media.

The Integrity Initiative was basically a ham-fisted British attempt to reproduce something along the lines of "Operation Mockingbird," the alleged 1950s CIA scheme that attempted to manipulate the U.S. news media for propaganda purposes. That particular plot apparently recruited many leading American journalists into its network, before it was exposed by journalists such as Seymour Hersh and Carl Bernstein of Watergate fame in the 1970s.

In more innocent times, Operation Mockingbird is said to have used tricks such as backing student and cultural groups, then utilizing them as front operations as well as recruiting some prominent American media figures into its network of propagandists.

Bernstein, in a 1977 *Rolling Stone* cover story, wrote that more than 400 American journalists had "secretly carried out assignments for the Central Intelligence Agency" in the 25 years proceeding his expose. The famed reporter asserted that "some of the most powerful organizations and individuals in American journalism" of that time were involved and that the likes of *The New York Times*, CBS television, and *Time* magazine had played ball with the spooks. Some wore their cooperation as a badge of honor. "I'm proud they asked me and proud to have done it," said Joseph Alsop, a popular syndicated columnist of the era.

The Institute for Statecraft's Integrity Initiative looked like a very amateurish attempt to reproduce something similar, albeit completely lacking the sophistication and guile of anything the CIA might attempt. It was essentially a platform run by incompetents, with an exaggerated sense of their own abilities, which was quietly put to sleep when it was clear they had made a hash of it.

Here's the gist of what it was all about. Basically, the British authorities earmarked £1,961,000 in 2018–19 (UK Parliament 2018), as part of a £100 million propaganda push over five years. Or, as they preferred to view it themselves, "producing important work to counter disinformation and other malign influence."

But the whole thing blew up in their faces when the organization's entire structure was leaked, or hacked, possibly by Russians, depending on who you believe.

Its focus was narrow, yet depressingly obvious—it went after Russia, specifically Russian media, Labour's Jeremy Corbyn, and Scottish nationalists. "Most boys grow out of spy games by their early teens," wrote Scotland's *Sunday Mail* in a stinging editorial. "There still exists into adulthood, however, a certain type who remain attracted to the idea of meeting in a dark corridor or on a park bench to counteract some insurgent political movement, real or imagined."

The Institute for Statecraft's Integrity Initiative was supposed to counter Russian online propaganda by forming "clusters" of friendly journalists and "key influencers" throughout Europe, which developed into an instrument to attack the political opposition in the UK. Just take a moment to breathe and think about it: a British government project smearing the country's most obvious alternative prime minister. The abuse included Corbyn being labeled "a useful idiot." Yet the London-based mainstream media essentially ignored the story, leaving it to a small Scottish newspaper to serve the truth to the public. In normal circumstances—and this is not hyperbole—the UK foreign office splurging millions of pounds on a cut-out designed to demean the opposition leader might even have been enough to bring down the government of the day. However, when the consequential press plays dumb, those conditions do not exist.

The Integrity Initiative was headed by one Chris Donnelly, a reserve officer in the British Army Intelligence Corps, who had once led the British Army's Soviet Studies Research Centre at Sandhurst. He was appointed an "Honorary Colonel in Military Intelligence" in 2015—the year the Integrity Initiative was formed, the *Mail* alleged.

The *Sunday Mail* took up the cudgel, explaining how "the Integrity Initiative has apparently left itself exposed to Russian hackers, fallen foul of Foreign Office rules, made itself the subject of an emergency question in the House of Commons and apparently broken charity law" in a strong April 2019 editorial (Daily Record 2019). "Just as serious are the concerns about the effectiveness of its actual activities," the piece continued. "They include the creation of clusters of media people, some who admit to being involved, others who don't. In one case they apparently took a briefing on Scotland which offered about as much insight as one could gather from a five-minute Google search."

Furthermore, the *Sunday Mail* revealed how "even after many of its flaws were exposed by this newspaper, its Twitter feed carried a smear attacking our journalists." So, here we had a British government-funded propaganda effort targeting an individual member of the press, and the London media did not find it worthy of coverage. Perhaps because many members of the capital city press cooperated with Integrity Initiative, which appears to be the case from the documents leaked online.

In November 2019, The Scottish Charity Regulator (OSCR) published the results of its investigation into the Integrity Initiative's parent, Institute for Statecraft. Its judgment was damning (OSCR 2019). The institute was considered to have failed the tests which define whether an organization can be classified as a charity, and it was also found that its trustees breached their duties, often seriously. Notably, as the inquiry took shape, "further concerns emerged" about the group.

A journalist observed that "when OSCR started digging they realized the troubling organization was even more troubling than first thought. For one, the Institute for Statecraft was not found to be serving a charitable purpose." While the Institute for Statecraft attempted to argue that its purposes were charitable, a review of public statements and internal documents made by the organization demonstrated this was nonsense. Moreover, the entire Integrity Initiative project was found to have "failed to provide public benefit."

The Integrity Initiative was also discovered to have "expressed a particular perspective intended to persuade the public to a specific point of view," also known as propaganda. The OSCR thus concluded it was a "propaganda/psyop outfit serving a particular interest." This is perhaps unsurprising as its directors had been involved in many dubious business ventures and tax arrangements in the past. The OSCR found that the Institute for Statecraft avoided leaving any paper trail as its activities were always to be kept secret.

When the OSCR findings were published, writer Tim Fenton noted that "the disinformation industry just lost a battle. But it has not yet lost the war." "In reality, it was all about Russophobia, trying to stoke fear of potential Russian actors and assets, even if they were not Russian actors or assets. It was perpetuating Cold War paranoia under another name. Which is where the Labour bashing came in," he observed. The Institute for Statecraft claimed to be "totally independent and impartial, not dependent on funding from political or government agencies." This was not true: it had received around £2 million from the Foreign Office during 2017/8 to run the Integrity Initiative. And the latter was then caught circulating anti-Jeremy Corbyn articles.

The story of the Integrity Initiative should have been a cautionary tale about how anti-Russian propaganda that served the purpose of establishing conformity around a foreign policy was instead used to attack domestic political opponents. The UK had a very similar experience in its own past. The Red Scare emerged in Britain in the 1920s and was directed against its own population to undermine the rise of the British labor movement.

The British Labour Party had emerged from the trade union movement of the late 19th century and offered entirely different political ideals that would upset the status quo. The Labour Party's first government was brought down in 1924 by fabricating links to the main out-group—the Soviet Union. A letter purportedly from Grigory Zinoviev, the head of the Communist International (Comintern), ordered the Communist Party of Britain to engage in subversive activities and mobilize sympathetic supporters within the Labour Party to support a treaty between Britain and the Soviet Union. The letter also specified that diplomatic relations between Moscow and the Labour government would contribute to the radicalization of the British working class, a conspiracy that would eventually spark a workers' revolution.

The *Daily Mail* printed the letter and the Labour Party predictably collapsed, with its credibility in tatters for years. The letter has been proven to be a forgery, intended to delegitimize the political opposition and harden anti-Russian sentiments. The letter was most likely written by Desmond Morten, an MI6 officer and close friend of Winston Churchill, and Major Joseph Ball, an MI5 officer, who later joined the Conservative Central Office (Bennett 2018). British intelligence agencies were at the center of the scandal, in collusion with some members of the Conservative Party and partisan members of the media.

13. The German Marshall Fund

The German Marshall Fund (GMF) of the United States has become increasingly prominent in recent years. Despite its name, the GMF is a very American body these days with little input from Berlin. It was founded by a donation from Willy Brandt's Bonn government to celebrate the 25th anniversary of the Marshall Plan. Ironically, Brandt is today best remembered as the father of "Ostpolitik," which sought a rapprochement between Germany and Russia.

After the fall of the Soviet Union, the GMF transformed into a vehicle promoting U.S. influence in Eastern Europe, with outreach in Warsaw, Belgrade, and Bucharest. However, it has recently taken a very strange turn. Following the election of U.S. President Donald Trump, the lobby group launched the Alliance for Securing Democracy (ASD) project. Its initial centerpiece was the "Hamilton 68 Dashboard," which seemed to classify social media users who reject the U.S. liberal elite's consensus as "Russian trolls." The reaction has been highly critical, with even the opaquely funded western-backed Russian-language website Meduza asking "how do you identify 'pro-Russian amplifiers' if... themes dovetail with alternative American political views?"

USAID are big backers, throwing in a seven-figure annual sum. This, of course, raises some questions about U.S. taxpayers essentially funding the Hamilton 68 dashboard, which may be smearing Americans who don't agree with their government's policies as Russian agents. The State Department also ponies up capital, as does

NATO and Latvia's Defense Ministry. Other interesting paymasters are George Soros, Airbus, and Google, while Boeing and the ubiquitous Raytheon are also involved.

14. The Legatum Institute

A British think tank deserving of attention is the Legatum Institute, a private lobby firm masquerading as an academic pursuit. The best synopsis of what Legatum does came in 2015, from the keyboard of Mark Ames, a veteran Russia correspondent. His focus was one particular lobbyist, Peter Pomerantsev. Ames's interest was spiked by why a "presumed journalist/writer like Pomerantsev" would be "lobbying the U.S. and UK governments to pass bills upping psychological warfare budgets and imposing sanctions on foreign countries?" Ames wrote:

> Legatum turns out to be a project of the most secretive billionaire vulture capital investor you've (and I'd) never heard of: Christopher Chandler, a New Zealander who, along with his billionaire brother Richard Chandler, ran one of the world's most successful vulture capital funds—Sovereign Global/Sovereign Asset Management. That family of funds, based in the offshore haven of Monaco, operated until 2004, when the Chandler brothers, Richard and Chris, divided their billions into two separate funds. . . . Christopher Chandler took his billions to Dubai, where he launched Legatum Capital, and, in 2007, the Legatum Institute.

Legatum for a number of years employed Anne Applebaum as a lobbyist and was also home to Cristina Odone, who just happens to be the wife of Edward Lucas. The think tank world is very, very small.

Anton Shekhovtsov lobbied for Legatum during the Ukraine crisis, when Applebaum and Pomerantsev were also attached, and the firm was running "info wars" around the conflict. In the mid-2000s, Shekhovtsov was involved with the International Eurasian Movement's youth wing in Crimea. Known as the "Eurasian Youth Union" (ECM in Russian), it is a right-wing organization that largely follows the teachings of Russian philosopher Alexander Dugin. In 2011, the organization was banned in Ukraine, after the Kiev government branded it an "extremist anti-Ukrainian organization." Back in 2006, Shekhovtsov was helping to organize an "anti-NATO weekend" in Sevastopol, Crimea's capital, which involved a "solemn procession along the city ring with flags and banners (of the Eurasian Movement)," according to contemporary accounts.

During the "festivities," Shekhovstov's comrades even managed to keep the place an EU-free zone. "The appearance of the blue flag of the Atlanticist European Union was suddenly noticed at the other end of the square," a report detailed. "A group of activists of the Young Guard and the ECM were immediately sent to him. And, because of peaceful negotiation, EU representatives left the square, frightened by the pressure of the Eurasian forces." Shekhovstov was present at the event, it is documented in photographs freely available online. Just eight years after Shekhovtsov stood against the West in Crimea, he found himself attached to Legatum, working as an "information warrior."

According to Ivan Katchanovski, Shekhovtsov was "cheering the mass killing of people in Odessa, whitewashing or denying far-right involvement in the Maidan, the Odessa massacre and the war in Donbas, and attacking scholars of the far-right in Ukraine actually benefited his info warrior career." By 2020, he was long gone from the Chandlers and had moved on to the "Free Russia Foundation," while also writing for Atlantic Council (again, the think tank racket is a village), as well as working as an external lecturer at the University of Vienna and a "senior fellow" at the "Free Russia Foundation."

In February of that year, he delivered more proof that the think tank business is little more than a cynical racket—if it were needed—with an op-ed that exposed the rot at the heart of the swindle. Even by the low standards of U.S./UK think tank grift, it was something else, running the full gamut of integrity from Y to Z. It also exposed the ambidextrous and duplicitous nature of much dogma in the former Soviet space, a part of the world where loyalties and worldviews can change utterly, depending on which direction the wind is blowing. In this case, Shekhovstov had flipped from promoting the philosophy of the ECM to sympathizing with Ukrainian fascists.

The Atlantic Council clearly wanted to protect the Azov Brigade from being designated a "foreign terrorist organization" in the U.S. A measure was suggested by Democratic Party Congressman Max Rose and former FBI agent Ali Soufan in a *New York Times* article where they dubbed the Ukrainian outfit "a paramilitary unit" notorious for its "association with neo-Nazi ideology."

Their primary concern was its association with other white supremacist groups worldwide. Azov's connections to this murky world are not in question. For instance, British investigation group Bellingcat, hardly a friend of Russia, describes it as a "Ukrainian white nationalist movement" which aspires to assist a "world conservative revolution," aiming to "defend the white race."

The official emblem of Azov is the wolfsangel in front of the black sun, two key symbols from Nazi Germany. Shekhovstov insisted the controversial group is part of the Ukrainian National Guard, overseen by the Ministry of Internal Affairs—as if this somehow makes its extremism more palatable. He then spent hundreds of words whitewashing Azov, with not so much of a mention of its predisposition for torchlight parades, and other events associated with Nazi symbolism. Indeed, even U.S. state broadcaster RFE/RL has reported on this sort of thing, dubbing Azov an "ultranationalist group" and a "fearsome far-right military force."

The Anglo-American think tank racket is a small, but lucrative, world, where decency, honesty, and probity are far from priorities. Yet, even allowing for this, the Atlantic Council reached a new low with that piece, leaving one to wonder if its biggest financial backers, such as Facebook and the British Foreign Office, which give it over $1 million annually, share its support of white supremacist neo-Nazi views.

15. HJS: The Henry Jackson Society

Similarly contrary in location to the German Marshall Fund, the Henry Jackson Society was set up in London and is highly influential in the media. It was set up in 2005, after being spawned at Peterhouse College, Cambridge. Among the signatories of its "Statement of Principles" was Sir Richard Dearlove, who as head of MI6 oversaw the intelligence failures which enabled the UK's role in the illegal invasion of Iraq.

Right from the start, the HJS' choice of name alone gave a clear indication of its agenda. Senator Jackson, a very illiberal U.S. politician who died in 1983, is best described as a sort of "patron saint" of neoconservatism. So much so that Paul Wolowitz, Bill Kristol, and Richard Perle, who were heavily associated with the movement, served as his aides during his lifetime (Griffin, Aked, Miller, and Marusek 2015). In England, the HJS is best known for its stout defense of Israel and has been accused of having an anti-Muslim outlook. Indeed, it even absorbed many members of a pro-Israeli media watchdog "Just Journalism," in 2011. Incidentally, one of those was Michael Weiss, who went on to ignite the "Russian disinformation" racket.

Guardian journalist Nafeez Ahmed (2014) accused HJS of courting "corporate, political power to advance a distinctly illiberal oil and gas agenda in [the] Mideast." Meanwhile, three years later the *Sunday Times* reported how HJS was being paid "about £10,000 a month by Japan to wage a propaganda campaign against China." The think tank had "encouraged politicians including the former foreign secretary Sir Malcolm Rifkind and journalists to voice opposition to Chinese foreign policy," the newspaper stated. (Kerbaj 2017).

Rifkind later appeared to confirm the story when he admitted to having been approached by the society to pen an article in the *Daily Telegraph* concerning China's involvement in Britain's Hinkley Point C nuclear plants (Connelly 2017). This, of course, is an especially blatant example of how the think tank racket has corrupted the mainstream media, given it what amounts to direct pay-for-play.

While HJS is incredibly powerful in terms of media influence, its ineptitude can frequently be amusing. One example comes from 2019 when Russian Ambassador Alexander Yakovenko stepped down and returned to Moscow. The *Daily Mail*, still Britain's best-selling non-tabloid top paper, sensationalized the exit under the headline "Russian ambassador to London who made mocking remarks about Salisbury poisoning is ordered home after revelations he worked as a Soviet spy."

The assertion was "backed up" by HJS' Andrew Foxall, dubbed director of its "Russia Studies Centre," who opined that since 1991, Russia's ambassadors in London have served either three or five-year terms. Mr. Yakovenko has served eight. Given that eight is not easily divisible by three or five, it seems unlikely from this perspective that his leaving is part of a scheduled change" (Lazarus 2019). Notwithstanding the fact that three plus five equals eight, which obviously means Yakovenko served two exact terms of different, but customary, lengths, the "Russia expert" seemed to be oblivious to Russian ambassadorial age limits—Russian law sets the age limit for civil servants at 65 years. While it can be extended in special circumstances, these obviously did not apply in Yakovenko's case.

Possibly the most ridiculous and shameless story that HJS was able to proliferate across the British media was its incredible research results on Russian spies in London. Fuelling the Russiagate hysteria, several British newspapers reported on the findings of HJS, concluding that "half of the Russians in London are spies." If so, then out of

150.000 Russians living in London, approximately 75.000 of them are supposedly Russian spies (Hope 2018).

While any self-respecting journalist would have picked up on the absurdity of such a claim, here, the story came from an "expert report." Furthermore, the *Times* informs that the story by HJS was supported by none other than Sir Richard Dearlove, the former head of MI6, although failing to mention he is also a signatory to the Henry Jackson Society's Statement of Principles. It is hardly a secret that standards at the *Times* are low. After all, the main foreign affairs columnist, Edward Lucas, is funded by U.S. weapons manufacturers. The *Times* does not make this conflict of interest clear to its readers. Another example of how the think tank's tail is wagging the mainstream media dog these days.

16. Chatham House

Chatham House, otherwise known as the Royal Institute of International Affairs, is probably most renowned for birthing the "Chatham House Rule," which, according to its own definition, means that after a debate "participants are free to use the information received, but neither the identity nor the affiliation of the speaker(s), nor that of any other participant, may be revealed."

That bit about the "affiliation of the speaker" is the most interesting part, because so much of the think tank racket operates on those principles as a general rule. After all, a "Senior Fellow at Chatham House" sounds prestigious and makes someone sound upstanding. But if the firm's sponsors were listed, people might form a different impression. In 2018/19, the famous London institution took six-figure sterling sums from George Soros and oil giants Chevron, Exxon Mobil, and Royal Dutch Shell, in addition to well over £2 million from the British government. And there were also payments from the ubiquitous U.S. National Endowment for Democracy, plus arms makers BAE Systems and Lockheed Martin.

Overall, it appears the biggest donor, by some distance, is the UK government. However, when a Chatham House "expert" is brought onto a media forum, it is simply never stated that most of their funding comes from the British state.

Nor does Chatham House outline the provenance of its speakers. For instance, Edward Lucas is a regular panelist on debates about

Eastern Europe, where he's listed as "Senior Vice-President, Center for European Policy Analysis; Columnist, The Times" (Chatham 2019). And this brings us once again to a key point. These foreign policy pundits may well passionately believe all they say, but why do they allow themselves to be attached to U.S. defense contractors? Especially given most of them have other irons in the fire, from which they presumably already draw a generous income.

It is the same story when they show up on the BBC. In the summer of 2018, the British State Broadcaster gave Lucas a "This Week" slot, replete with video for online consumption, to encourage European states to cooperate better on defense matters because "without American protection, we will have to hang together, otherwise we will hang separately" (BBC 2018). This was in response to U.S. President Donald Trump supposedly indicating "the U.S. will no longer pick up the bulk of the tab for NATO." In reality, Trump was trying to get European members of the alliance he was leading to spending more on weapons and other defense needs.

17. Think Tanks in the Countering Disinformation Industry

In the past, the path toward objective truths entailed open and critical debate. Open discourse was the instrument to expose weak arguments that could not be substantiated, while strong and sensible arguments enabled credible analysts and publishers to climb the meritocracy ladder. The disinformation hysteria of recent years has resulted in a departure from this practice by instead establishing "fact-checkers" as gatekeepers for what is deemed to be correct and thus monopolizing what is taken to be true. In this new system, censorship is now billed not an attack on democracy but a necessary instrument to preserve it. The efforts to discredit Russian media laid the foundation for the decision to impose censorship across the West, and most particularly against Russian media outlets such as RT and Sputnik after the Russian invasion of Ukraine in 2022.

In George Orwell's *1984*, a Ministry of Truth is tasked to decide what is truth and what are lies, which our current fact-checker industry begins to resemble. Whoever obtains the role as a gatekeeper can determine the truth, thereby bestowing upon that person or entity immense power. Almost two centuries ago, Alexis de Tocqueville (2003: 162) cautioned in his work, *Democracy in America*, that creating a government body with the power to assess the truth in media would create tyranny:

> Whoever should be able to create and maintain a tribunal of this kind would waste his time in prosecuting the liberty of the press; for he would be the absolute master of the whole community and would be as free to rid himself of the authors as of their writings.

Disinformation is a real problem, and there is certainly a demand for organizations that can explore the alleged facts presented in the media. However, the present development demonstrates that fact-checking is outsourced to ideological and interest-based organizations. Furthermore, these organizations often check narratives as opposed to facts. Think tanks are in the business of exerting influence through controlling information, which makes them natural contenders for the role of gatekeepers and fact-checkers.

In Britain and the United States, among other markets, tabloid newspapers have published plenty of rubbish for decades, and few batted an eyelid. It was generally understood that news from "red-tops" was broadly less accurate than what you would expect from the "respectable press."

Nevertheless, the scandal sheets have long outsold their more serious brethren. For instance, in the United Kingdom, the *Sun* has around ten times the circulation of the *Guardian*. Meanwhile, in Germany, *Bild* is, by some distance, the market leader. And it is not only in the West; the Russian newspaper market is dominated by *Komsomolskaya Pravda* and *Moskovski Komsomolets*. Presumably, because the leading tabloids tend to be heavily pro-establishment, governments and policy advisories have pretty much left them alone. Even when they have been foreign-owned. For example, the aforementioned *Sun* is controlled by Rupert Murdoch, an Australian. But rather than attempt to clip Murdoch's wings, London's politicians have sought his support. Tony Blair, notably, went to extraordinary lengths to persuade Murdoch to switch his backing from the Conservatives to the 1990s "New Labour" project.

So, because the rags are not seen as a threat to the established order, and are often a way to secure working-class support for policies pushed by the powers that be, they are tolerated. Thus, "disinformation" has only become an issue in recent years, as a handful of foreign-owned news outlets punch a few holes in the traditional Anglo-American domination of English-language media that are larger than the limited capacity of the marginalized independent media.

That these "info warriors" have an agenda is evidenced by the fact that they rarely, if ever, focus on the Anglo-American media, which, objectively speaking, carries more porkies in a day than the much smaller Russian media could manage in a few months. Of course, many (almost always government-funded) who purport to be "fighting disinformation" are often far more efficient in that dark art than the media outlets they obsess over. This is what makes this "disinformation" business basically a lucrative racket.

The Decline of U.S./UK Information Dominance

Information dominance remains a central aspect of great power politics after the Cold War. The U.S. aims to advance and cement the unipolar moment through "total spectrum dominance" and recognised the need for information dominance. The Pentagon's *Joint Vision 2020* outlined the objective that "U.S. forces are able to conduct prompt, sustained and synchronized operations with combinations of forces tailored to specific situations and with access to and freedom to operate in all domains—space, sea, land, air and information." Paradoxically, information dominance enables the U.S. to appear to have an open society due to the illusion of dissent in the media. Dissent can be tolerated to a greater extent when the government can control and narrow the scope of acceptable opinions. When information dominance is lost, the U.S. becomes more reliant on crude efforts to limit speech and opposition (Miller 2004: 9).

The challenge to information dominance began after the Cold War. Initially, the foundation in 1996 of a Qatari-state-backed cable news network, Al Jazeera, began the disruption. Before the Emir of Qatar funded its start-up, the Arab world had lacked a global voice of its own. Then, as researcher Megan Zingarelli memorably put it, Al Jazeera "ended the flow of information that followed the format of from the 'West to the rest.'" Nevertheless, despite its relatively balanced output, several western competitors dismissed the channel as a mouthpiece for the terrorist group Al Qaeda and various Middle Eastern despots.

Al Jazeera almost stood alone in ruffling feathers for some time, and even by the mid-2000s, there were still few news-orientated products with real worldwide reach. In the print sphere, you had the likes of *The Economist* (London), *Time*, and *Newsweek*. Meanwhile, the world's hotel bedrooms were mainly served by America's CNN, and the British BBC.

Then, over just a few years, internet speeds dramatically increased and social media mushroomed from seemingly out of nowhere. Quickly, "the Al Jazeera effect" was in full swing. Suddenly, the rest of the world sensed an opportunity. Specialized offerings, such as *Le Monde Diplomatique* or Voice of Russia (previously Radio Moscow), had been around for years, but the new reality created conditions where mass-market penetration was possible.

In 2004, Germany's most influential magazine, *Der Spiegel*, launched an English-language website. This move was notable because it represented a heavyweight private brand expanding its horizons. However, it was state-backed initiatives that would make the biggest noise. And, as a consequence, upset the traditional gate-keepers. In a short period, new projects mushroomed. They included Press TV (Iran, 2007), RT (Russia, 2005), and France 24 (2006). All were, at least initially, clones of Al Jazeera to some degree. But the growth of these outlets was about to provide huge opportunities for expansion of the think tank racket, as specialists in some of those regions, previously restricted to the fringes, sensed the opportunity to rebrand as "info warriors."

Take a moment to think about where the average Russia wonk was in 2012. The Dmitry Medvedev presidency had led to a thaw in relations between Moscow and the West. Obama's U.S. had offered a "reset" in relations, and the Kremlin even proved flexible on a number of Western initiatives, most notably the 2011 intervention in Libya. This all meant slim pickings for the think tank racket because a friendly Russia is not profitable in their industry. This is partially because Moscow itself is not a source of funding, but it is also a consequence of the oversized contribution of arms makers and defense agencies to the budgets of these lobby groups.

Deutsche Welle (Germany) and Al Jazeera had steady reaches and were moderately successful and France 24 was doing reasonably well. However, there was one outlier. During the interregnum years (2009–2012), the reach of Russia's RT had managed to surge ahead of the other newbies, especially on YouTube. This was achieved by offering a platform to alternative voices from the West, who had largely been denied access to the Western mainstream. The launch of RT responded to a recognition that the international media was dominated by the U.S. and the UK, which are renowned for purveying a critical and hostile view of Russia. Russian Foreign Minister Sergey Lavrov (2007) argued that Russia's position is often misunderstood or ignored as "Russia is apparently not as skillful as the West when it comes to matters of communication." Putin (2012) similarly noted that Russia's main adversaries have a near monopoly on presenting Russia to the world:

> Russia's image abroad is formed not by us and as a result it is often distorted and does not reflect the real situation in our country. . . . Those who fire guns and launch air strikes here or there are the good guys, while those who warn of the need for restraint and dialogue are for some reason at fault. But our fault lies in our failure to adequately explain our position.

This, of course, was seen by some as a threat to the traditional media order. Thus, the idea of Russia operating some sort "hybrid war" through media was born. The rise of alternative sources of information incentivized Washington to reverse the decline of its dominance in the information space. Towards this end, Hillary Clinton requested more funding for the "information war":

> During the Cold War we did a great job in getting America's message out. After the Berlin Wall fell we said, "Okay, fine, enough of that, we are done," and unfortunately we are paying a big price for it. Our private media cannot fill that gap . . . we are in an information war. And we are losing that war. (U.S. Senate 2011: 17).

NATO's Deputy Assistant Secretary-General for Public Diplomacy, Stephanie Babst (2010: 1), similarly emphasized the "ever-greater need for well-planned public diplomacy efforts. Strategic communications, branding, and public affairs are widely seen as essential tools to win over the hearts and minds of foreign audiences."

The idea that Moscow is running some sort of sophisticated, well-thought-out, strategy to undermine the western point of view, is complete balderdash. In reality, RT is a young organization staffed by a bunch of people trying to do their best to cover the news. Most sections are pretty much autonomous, with no heavy hand dictating from above. Veteran broadcaster Larry King, who himself hosted a program on the network, argued that RT "is one of the few channels doing news" (Burch 2018). What King meant is that U.S. networks have switched to personality-driven coverage and opinion, while the Moscow-based alternative is mostly just reporting facts.

RT does not hide that it presents a Russian view on developments in the world, much like as can be seen in the domestic orientation of its counterparts in other states. RT, therefore, provides a valuable contribution as the Russian perspective is largely absent from the American and British media. The ongoing Western information war reduces the pluralism of perspectives in Western media, which is necessary for an informed audience. Information wars are harmful to open societies as they create a conflict between the ideal and practice of democratic debate and the state's need to mobilize opinion against the hostile power.

To understand Russian policies, it is necessary to discuss its security interests and the threat to these interests. But when was the last time any of us opened a Western newspaper where the reasonability of

Russia having security interests was even discussed? If we cannot discuss threats Russia faces from the West, then all Russian policies must be presented as if they were occurring in a vacuum—caused solely by internal issues in within Russia. Accordingly, all Russian policies can thus be explained by the malign character of Putin, the Russian fear of democracy, or its desire to restore a Soviet empire. Removing the West's actions as a variable among factors underlying a situation produces dangerous policies. When we recognize competing security interests, peace can be promoted with understanding and compromise, but if conflicts are wilfully interpreted as good versus evil values, then understanding and compromise are equated with defeat and appeasement, as tacitly, lasting peace requires instead that good triumphs over evil.

The Disinformation Warrior

The effort to deprive Russian media of legitimacy began to some extent with a 2013 report from Peter Pomerantsev and Michael Weiss, a pair of think tankers engaged by the family of one-time oil-magnate Mikhail Khodorkovsky, while he was still imprisoned in Russia on controversial tax evasion charges. Their thesis suggested the Kremlin was "weaponizing information." And, with that, a new trope was born.

The Weiss/Pomerantsev report was blessed by its timing. As tensions between Russia and the West ratcheted up over Ukraine and Syria, it suited the mood of the day and essentially spawned an industry. From it, the think tank racket birthed a new sort of charlatan for the late 2010s: "the disinformation" warrior. The approach was rather effective as any arguments and stories that emerged from Russian media could be denounced as propaganda or disinformation, without bothering to substantiate the allegation.

To become a disinformation or hybrid war expert, all you needed to do was to fling around a few Russian terms, such as dezinformatsiya (disinformation itself) and kompromat (compromising material), and hysterically denounce Westerners engaging with Russian media, and you were all set.

By 2019, U.S. state media's RFERL, NATO's Atlantic Council adjunct, and the European Union were all funding infowars cutouts. This has created a problem in itself. So many people have now been hired as specialists in this snake oil that there is the question of what to do with them if the tide or the Western focus ever changes. What, then, will think tanks do with all these "hybrid warfare" experts?

The Counter-Propaganda Industry

Propaganda aims to control the narrative, and is thus commonly concealed under the rubric of counter-propaganda, perhaps viewed as a more effective instrument to censor the opponent's arguments. Bertrand Russell (1932: 139–40) argued that propaganda entails circumventing reason and aims to "close the mind to argument," which infers that countering propaganda requires elevating reason by opening the mind to all perspectives. Russell therefore advocated countering propaganda by organizing debates between Churchill and the Soviet Ambassador, Gandhi and Viceroy, and Stalin and the Archbishop of Canterbury.

However, propaganda concealed as counter-propaganda instead aims to limit the exposure to counter-arguments and rational debate in order to control the narrative and monopolize what is viewed as truth. The propagandist does not aim to expose the weaknesses of the argument to their counterpart by exposing it to open discourse; instead the objective is to label the counterpart as providing dangerous propaganda from which the population must be protected through censorship.

Harold Lasswell (1995: 22), one of the main theorists of propaganda from the 1920s, argued that our propaganda is a key instrument against foreign propaganda: "The only effective weapon against propaganda on behalf of one policy seems to be propaganda on behalf of an alternative."

The former Director of the U.S. Information Agency's Office to Counter Soviet Disinformation and Active Measures defined counter-propaganda as "carefully prepared answers to false propaganda with the purpose of refuting the disinformation and undermining the propagandist" (Romerstein 2009: 137). Senate Foreign Relations Committee, Assistant Secretary Victoria Nuland (2015) similarly called for greater information control to counter Russia:

> To fight disinformation not only in Ukraine and Russia, but across Russian-speaking communities in Europe, we are joining forces with our partners in the EU to support alternatives to state-sponsored Russian programming. We are also training foreign journalists and civil society actors in the art of fighting lies with the truth.

The EU proclaims it counters Russian propaganda by supporting media in its "eastern neighborhood" to denounce Russian disinformation and instead persuade people about the benefits of European-style reforms. Making the plea to develop mechanisms to counter Russian disinformation, the British Foreign Secretary Dominic Raab argued that "Pro-Russian trolls are posting comments on Ukraine and other areas, both to influence opinion here but to be played back in the Russian media," which should be countered by mechanisms to "provide a rebuttal—and frankly to provide the truth—for the people of this country but also in Russia or China or around the world" (RFE/RL 2021a).

Both the U.S. and the EU have established fact-checkers who aim to control the narrative by checking narratives rather than facts. Case in point: EU fact-checkers label the reference to the toppling of President Yanukovich of Ukraine in 2014 as a "coup" as Russian disinformation insofar as the EU has labeled it a "democratic revolution." The inconvenient facts they could check would be: Was the democratically elected president of Ukraine forced to flee due to the threat of violence? Did the protests, riots, or removal of the Ukrainian president from power result from a democratic process or have support from the majority of the Ukrainian population? Did the removal of the Ukrainian president violate the Ukrainian constitution? Were foreign players involved? All these objective facts are not favorable to the EU, thus they contest the narrative by presenting an ambiguous concept of "democratic revolution."

Repudiating fake news is openly equated to defending Western narratives and interests as, for example, leading EU officials advocated combating fake news to counter "populist rhetoric" and ensure that EU-sceptics "don't win at the ballot boxes" (Williams 2018). Robinson (2022) observes that the "disinformation industry" may be a cure worse than the disease, as fact-checkers have become sources of disinformation presenting unsubstantiated opinions as facts and denouncing perspectives favorable to Russia as fake news.

Fact-Checking "European Values"

Back in November 2017, one such outfit, the Czech-based "European Values," published what it called the "Prague Declaration," proposing "seven urgent steps" to be taken "to stop Russian aggression." The lobbyists claimed their petition was endorsed by "more than 100 European and American security experts and parliamentarians from 22 countries." It included many usual suspects like Bill Browder (a one-time Putin-supporting financier who transformed into a vociferous anti-Kremlin voice after his business in Russia was impeded) and Gary Kasparov (Soviet chess hero-turned-political-agitator), plus a litany of names from the EU think tank merry-go-round.

Just a month earlier, the same Prague lobbyists had made fools of themselves with a 52-page report labeling various people as "useful idiots" for appearing on the RT channel. Harrison Ford, Evander Holyfield, Mr. T, Oliver Stone, Stephen Fry, and Vivienne Westwood were among the famous showbiz folk targeted in a collection of 2,327 names. And they were joined by Kofi Annan, Mikhail Gorbachev, Peter Sutherland, Jeremy Corbyn, and Wolfgang Ischinger from the world of politics.

The compilation made some comical mistakes, such as confusing British Prime Minister Boris Johnson with an actor impersonating him and naming Noam Chomsky as "Noah." Even more bizarrely, it mistook the legendary Larry King for the equally illustrious Larry David. Not once, but dozens of times. These mistakes were made even more notable by the diatribe's opening call that "politicians and media organizations should publicly [sic] commit to a higher degree of fact-checking rigor." The fallacy of the alleged "fact-checking" becomes all too obvious.

Interestingly, European Values did omit some names of previous RT guests from its 2,327 "useful idiots" such as Julia Davis (Atlantic Council) and Eric Garland (promoter of the debunked "Russiagate" conspiracy, which alleged Donald Trump colluded with the Kremlin), who later transformed into anti-Russia critics. These contributors to RT were seemingly absolved for their sin of speaking to Russian media. This was picked up on by the Canadian journalist Michael Colborne, who noted "this is just intellectually dishonest horseshit. Framing every single person ever on RT as an idiot . . . except your friends, conveniently" (MacDonald 2017).

So who paid for this nonsense? Well, quite possibly, you did. Depending on where you are located. Of the €4.3 million "European Values" received in 2017, much of it came from state bodies. The British taxpayer gave almost €950,000 (via the Foreign Office and the UK embassy in Prague), the European Parliament & Commission handed over €370,000, and the U.S. government paid €211,000 directly. Germany chipped in with €75,000 and NATO found €67,000. Even Israel found itself on the hook for €27,000.

All this money is for output which would embarrass first-year students at a decent third-level college. However, the meritocracy of the fact-checking industry is not based on presenting accurate facts; rather climbing the ladder depends on conforming with the correct narrative. The author of the useful idiots report, Monika Richter, does not appear to have been badly hurt by the missteps in the report. As of summer 2019, the Oxford graduate is employed at the EU's East Stratcom Task Force, which runs the aforementioned "EUvsDisinfo" project. Richter's progress proves another truism of the think tank racket. Even when its footsoldiers make blunders and gaffes for which mere mortals suffer, it seems to have no effect on their future prospects. Because being on message is more important than being right. As a result, few fall down. Instead, most fall up.

The "Disinformation Governance Board" and Its Appointed Director, Nina Jankowicz

Since the "disinformation" scare racket kicked off, one thing has become very apparent: those who scream most loudly about it are often its biggest curators.

The media is very selective in fact-checking, which tends to omit think tanks that spread "good disinformation." In late September 2019, *The Washington Post* gave over op-ed space in its Sunday edition to a piece by Nina Jankowicz (2019), a lobbyist at the U.S.-government-funded think tank, ostensibly designed to bust "myths" about Ukraine, which was full of false statements. This took place around the time of the Donald Trump-Rudy Giuliani-Joe Biden scandal, which led to impeachment proceedings against the U.S. President and dominated the news cycle for a long time.

That much of her piece was largely untrue is not a great surprise, because think-tankers and their agendas have been hogging *WAPO*'s op-ed pages for years. It is important to assess this article by Jankowicz because this fellow at the Wilson Center went on to take the position as president of the "Disinformation Governance Board" established by the Biden administration. Jankowicz was a cheerleader for the Trump-Russia Russiagate conspiracy theory and had worked towards legitimizing the Steele Dossier. In 2020, she dismissed the *New York Post*'s reporting of the Hunter Biden laptop as a "Trump campaign product," thus legitimizing censorship of the report.

In September 2021, one year after it had denounced the Hunter Biden story as Russian disinformation in the midst of the U.S. presidential election, Politico finally published an admission confirming the authenticity of the key emails from Hunter Biden's laptop that had been the most incriminating (Lizza, Bade, Palmeri and Daniels 2021). The evidence and admission of authenticity were remarkable as it is proved that the intelligence agencies, the tech giants, and the media had engaged in censorship to bury an authentic story that could have made Joe Biden lose the election, by dismissing it as Russian disinformation without any evidence to back that decision. Yet despite that, the Biden administration proceeded to make Nina Jankowicz the president of the Disinformation Governance Board.

Eventually Jankowicz had to withdraw from the position due to complaints from the conservatives about her partisanship and disinformation. Then, the Disinformation Governance Board was also dissolved after it was frequently compared to George Orwell's "Ministry of Truth."

What made her 2019 article so remarkable was the sheer depth of the deception and the fact *The Washington Post* clearly did not even bother with basic fact-checking. First off, readers were told that Ukraine is not to be called "the Ukraine." And this is absolutely fair. Purely because "the" suggests Ukraine is not an independent entity, the article reasoned, and is instead an appendage of something else. Like for instance, Crimea, which is commonly referred to as "the Crimea." (One wonders how applicable that argument is, take the case of The Netherlands. . . .) Nonetheless, Jankowicz was therefore correct to state "the country's official name is Ukraine" and assert how "leaders, journalists, and pundits should use it."

Sadly, it all went downhill from there. The fabrications kicked off with the notion that "Crimeans want(ing) to be part of Russia" was a "myth." Jankowicz claimed that in 2014 Russian troops "rolled into Ukraine's Crimean Peninsula and began wresting control of military installations and administrative resources from local authorities." In reality, the Russian troops had already been stationed there, so they did not "roll in." Furthermore, almost all Ukrainian military stationed in Crimea did not resist. So, there was no need to "wrest control." In fact, as Reuters reported, a large percentage of Ukrainian soldiers on the peninsula defected as soon as the opportunity presented itself (Polityuk and Zverev 2017). This included around 50 percent of local commanding officers, according to the then deputy chief of the Ukrainian armed forces' general staff, Alexander Rozmaznin (BBC 2014c). Every independent poll reaffirmed that the overwhelming majority of Crimea desired unification with Russia, and following the referendum in Crimea, approximately 75 percent of Ukraine's naval personnel defected to Russia or quit the Ukrainian navy (Greer and Shtekel 2020).

Jankowicz went on to claim that "the Kremlin has restricted access to the peninsula since its annexation, making it difficult to assess people's true sentiments." There were numerous opinion polls carried out between 2014–2019 that she might have been accepted as authoritative, but Jankowicz chose not to cite any of them, presumably because they would derail her narrative. And *The Washington Post* editors obviously did not pull her up on it either.

For instance, in the spring of 2014, only two months after 23 years of Kiev's rule had effectively ended, the U.S. state broadcaster BBG (since renamed USAGM and the parent of RFE/RL and Voice of America), in conjunction with American pollster Gallup, found that 82.8% of those surveyed believed the Crimea referendum (labeled "a sham" by Jankowicz) "reflected the views of most Crimeans." Furthermore, 73.9% felt rejoining Russia would have a "positive impact on their lives" (BBG 2014). A month later, Pew Research, another famed American pollster, reported that only seven percent of Crimeans thought the "Ukrainian government respects personal freedoms." Also, a whopping 91 percent insisted the vote to return to Russia was "free and fair" and 88 percent wanted Kiev to recognize the results (Pew 2014).

As reported by *Forbes*, when asked "do you endorse Russia's annexation of Crimea?," a total of 82 percent of respondents answered "yes, definitely," and another 11 percent answered, "yes, for the most part." Only two percent said they did not know, and another two percent said no. Three percent did not specify their position. Only one percent of Crimeans felt the Ukrainian media "provides entirely truthful information." *Forbes* recognized that all polls demonstrated that Ukrainians, ethnic Russians, and Tatars in Crimea are all overwhelmingly supportive of having transitioned from Ukraine to Russia (Rapoza 2015).

Yet again, in 2017, ZOiS, a research institute bankrolled by the German Foreign Ministry carried out another poll. It showed that "86 percent of non-Tatar respondents" reckoned another referendum would produce the same result. As did the majority of Tatars themselves, who make up about 12 percent of the local population. These were all Western surveys which cannot be dismissed as "Russian propaganda." Yet, Jankowicz completely ignored them.

Even more damningly, in the very same week, Oleg Sentsov told a U.S. state-funded television network operating in Ukraine that "after 20 years [of rule by Kiev], Russia was more comfortable than Ukraine [for Crimeans]. You can try to deny it, but it's a fact." This is the same Oleg Sentsov awarded the 2018 "Sakharov Prize" by the European Union for "freedom of thought," who served a prison sentence in Russia for Crimea-related terrorism charges, which he insists were without foundation.

Jankowicz also insisted that there was no civil war in Ukraine, because Russia supported separatists in the East, and there are allegations that Russian soldiers fought alongside them, while the United States supplied lethal weapons to Kiev and Ukrainian soldiers received training from NATO. While it is undoubtably true that Russia and NATO intereferred extensively in Ukraine, the crisis also has a strong domestic component. The conflict has two layers as a divided country in a divided Europe, and the framing of the conflict is thus important in the information war. Presenting it solely as a conflict between Ukraine and Russia has the effect of depriving Eastern Ukrainians of agency and neglecting the key role of NATO, although, on the Russia side there is similarly a tendency to ignore the agency of Ukraine by focusing excessively on NATO and the fascist elements in the Ukrainian government.

Nevertheless, even if Russia (or the U.S.) had openly dispatched a few thousand troops to the front line, or provided air support, it would actually have remained a "Civil War" as this has become an accepted application of the term, even where there were considerable amounts of foreign involvement, such as the Syria and Yemen conflicts, which are still known as "Civil Wars," and the Spanish Civil War of the 20th century, in which the German Luftwaffe and Italian Aviazione Legionaria bombed civilians from the skies and the Soviet Union (of which Ukraine was then a member) had committed thousands of personnel.

Then there's the Russian Civil War of 1917–22, which featured foreign interventions by Britain, Japan, the U.S., France, Italy, China, and more than ten other states, yet it is still classed as a Civil War.

As the Canadian-Ukrainian academic, Ivan Katchanovski, has noted: "The denial of the civil war in Ukraine is fake news, aka classic disinformation and propaganda." His research has shown that over 94 percent of the combatants exchanged in prisoner swaps with separatists or Russia by Ukraine, during the five years of fighting were Ukrainian citizens.

Another "myth" Jankowicz attempted to debunk was the idea that Ukraine "is hopelessly corrupt," despite pointing to government "progress" in battling graft, citing the implementation of an "online procurement system for government tenders." Well, corruption is difficult to measure. The best-known index, from Germany's Transparency International, judges Ukraine very harshly, but as it is based on "perceptions of corruption," it is hard to actually quantify, making it an unfair metric. At the same time, well known Ukrainian politician and journalist Sergey Leshchenko, who is something of a Western media darling, told the BBC (2016) that corruption "is Ukraine's number one problem, it has to be stopped."

Interestingly, the Atlantic Council (2019) admitted how between 2014-19, the Petro Poroshenko administration in Kiev had:

- "not dismantled Ukraine's corrupt system of government or taken on the oligarchy"
- "not upheld the rule of law by removing corrupt judges, police or prosecutors, and replacing them with bullet-proof law enforcement institutions"
- "not protected reform-minded ministers or officials from harassment or obstacles by oligarchs, corrupt government officials, larcenous politicians, and organized crime"
- "failed to create and protect a free and unfettered press by forcing oligarchs, criminals, and powerful vested interests to divest their media assets"
- "failed to instigate or support the removal of immunity for members of parliament, who 'sell' their seats and votes which is the basis of political corruption in the country."

It was a pretty damning assessment, which flew in the face of Jankowicz's claim that "the progress since the rejection of the corrupt Yanukovych regime in 2014 is unmistakable." The main issue we want to bring to attention here was the failure of *The Washington Post* to apply even basic standards of fact-checking before publication. That makes it serve as a fine example of how the think tank racket now dominates opinion writing in establishment media.

The Atlantic Council Enters the Disinformation Industry

In the summer of 2018, Atlantic Council decided to leap into the "disinformation" industry in earnest, with a typically slick website. Dubbed the "DisInfoPortal," it actually kicked off with a bit of deception of its own. Right on the landing page, which told visitors that "in 2014, Putin invaded Ukraine, the first annexation of territory in Europe since World War II," a contention that we have debunked, above. This came replete with animated tanks powering across the image (RT 2018). This meant that the Atlantic Council ignored the events of 1974 when (NATO member!) Turkey staged a de-facto annexation of Northern Cyprus, a military occupation that continues to this day. Of course, the "think tank" receives money from the Turkish government too, via the state-owned Turkish Petroleum Corporation, as mentioned above.

Indeed, if you really wanted to be pedantic, you could point to Britain's 1955 annexation of Rockall, which was enshrined in legislation in 1972, despite objections from Ireland, which still conducts occasional naval patrols exercising what it perceives as its sovereign rights (Heffernan 2012).

The Atlantic Council was able to hire over 80 "experts" for its project. They included some of the usual suspects who circulate around the think tank racket—Eliot Higgins is there and Alina Polyakova. Ben Nimmo, too, and Brian Whitmore. Edward Lucas is also attached, along with Andrew Weisburd and Michael Weiss. However, the team member of greatest interest is Julia Davis. In the autumn of 2019, Davis, a Ukrainian immigrant to the U.S., was probably the most influential person covering Russia or Ukraine in English-language

Twitter. This would have been a significant achievement if she had put her status to constructive use. But, sadly, she did not. Essentially, Davis watched Russian TV shows, then took comments by pundits and twisted them, presenting them as indications of official Russian policy. A coalition of eager members of the anti-Trump "resistance" and diehard anti-Russia activists promoted her work and helped her secure a six-figure following, along with think tank stalwart Anne Applebaum, a particularly enthusiastic supporter.

That October, Sergey Radchenko, a Welsh-based academic originally from Russia, pointed out how the lobbyist was actually spreading falsehoods herself under the Atlantic Council banner. Davis claimed: "Russia's state TV program hosted by notorious propagandist Vladimir Soloviev—who is close to Putin and has special access to the Kremlin—spends 30 minutes extolling Tulsi Gabbard, arguing she should be 'the face of the Democratic party' and obsessively bashing Hillary Clinton." However, Radchenko smelt a rat and viewed the segment himself and commented: "Just out of curiosity, I watched this program by Vladimir Soloviev." Radchenko continued "There is nothing there that remotely looks like 'extolling' Tulsi Gabbard (nor is she called 'the face of the Democratic Party'). Nor did I find any obsessive bashing of HRC" (Hillary Clinton). "When Gabbard is discussed, it's just to ridicule the notion that she is a Russian 'asset,' as no one seems to know much about her," he continued.

Davis, who has been published in *The Washington Post* and the Daily Beast, presumably because of the legitimacy the Atlantic Council grants her, has thread quite the path to mainstream recognition. Before becoming interested in Russia-related "info wars," she appeared on RT, and various other media outlets, alleging the late actress Brittany Murphy was murdered by the U.S. government and had also targeted Davis because she knew too much. Murphy, the ex-girlfriend of Hollywood A-lister Ashton Kutcher, died in 2009, aged only 32. Davis was the focus of a lengthy *Huffington Post* article that set out the case for her theory and also talked about Alex Jones' Info Wars, outlining her belief that the U.S. government murders its own citizens (Flint 2012). Yet, just a few years later, the Atlantic Council repackaged and rebranded her as a "Russian media expert." A cynical move that says more about NATO's propaganda adjunct than Davis herself.

Chatham House in the Disinformation Industry

Chatham House's fervently anti-Russia standpoint often sees it pressuring other groups it considers "soft" on Moscow. In April 2020, a report from British academics revealed how "claims by the EU's diplomatic service that RT is spreading fake news about the coronavirus pandemic were misleading and based on bad methodology." It came after many mainstream U.S./UK media outlets uncritically parroted allegations from East StratCom—and its EUvsDisinfo information war wing—that "Russian pro-Kremlin media" was conducting a "significant disinformation campaign" to stoke "confusion, panic and fear" in the West and "aggravate the coronavirus pandemic crisis."

"The extent of EUvsDisinfo's misrepresentation of Russian Covid-19 media coverage is troubling," wrote the report's authors, Stephen Hutchings and Vera Tolz, professors of Russian Studies at the University of Manchester. They noted how "there is little evidence of systematic disinformation in RT's Covid-19 reporting. Despite some deficient practices much of the output was factual, consisting of aggregated Western news agencies reports." They also warned that "careless 'counter-disinformation' research can become a source for disinformation itself, skewing policy decisions in the EU and the UK," before noting that, in terms of Covid-19 coverage, RT's reporting practices "are undoubtedly superior to East StratCom's own methods."

East StratCom is part of the EEAS (the EU's diplomatic corps) and is designed to spread Brussels' message/propaganda in Armenia, Azerbaijan, Belarus, Georgia, Moldova, and Ukraine—countries Eurocrats have long wanted to pull into their orbit—as well as in Russia itself. Its EUvsDisinfo project is an absurd "information wars" racket, where a large number of its 3,000 contributors clearly hold strongly negative views of Russia. "Such volunteers, moreover, are operating in a post-Soviet space saturated (for very understandable reasons) by anti-Russian sentiments from which they are unlikely to be completely free," Hutchings and Tolz noted. "By outsourcing vital research to volunteers working in ideologically fraught environments, EUvsDisinfo will inevitably struggle to present reliable, robust findings."

Its output often entails labeling huge chunks of Russian-language comment or reportage as the views of the Russian state. The process is as ludicrous as having some media monitor in Moscow watching the BBC, ITV, and Sky, or listening to LBC and various local radio stations, then jotting down every guest's opinion as representative of London's official outlook. Yet, bureaucrats and politicians who do not have expertise on Russia often take EUvsDisinfo at face value. This leads to distrust and helps strain relations. A couple of years ago, the Dutch government wanted it shut down, but it still staggers on.

The research by Tolz and Hutchings upset a lot of the usual suspects in the think tank racket. After all, a lot of people are doing very well due to their participation in the "disinformation industry," and it has brought new vigor and funding to the think-tank racket. Predictably, many of them circled like vultures on social media, tearing into the posters.

Keir Giles, a think tanker at Chatham House, responded with an article titled "Defence Against Disinformation is a Team Sport," which begins by suggesting that counter-disinformation initiatives should avoid friendly fire. Giles concludes that "mutual support is overdue: by seeking a cooperative, rather than adversarial, approach between players on the same side, defenders against malign influence can help mitigate the effects of propaganda outlets rather than providing them with material." In other words, the lobbyist is telling Hutchings and Tolz not to break ranks in the future and to remember which side they are supposed to be representing. Even if that side is clearly shooting itself in the foot by spreading "disinformation" in the name of fighting against it. He was also upset that RT reported on the report of Tolz and Hutchings about EUvsDisinfo.

In short, he took more than 3,300 words to imply what he clearly meant: that objectivity in the evaluation of Russian media could derail a gravy train that is keeping a lot of people in well-paid employment. After all, once decision-makers realize that the "Russian disinformation" racket is a mighty con, the cash spigot will quickly turn off, and its practitioners will be left with a redundant set of "skills." They will not exactly be inundated with offers of work.

18. Think Tanks and the Media

The democracy and civil rights movement of the 1960s undermined elite control over the political culture and the media. The Trilateral Commission was established in 1973 to bolster cooperation between North America, Western Europe and Japan. The subsequent report on the "governability of democracies" identified that "some of the problems of governance in the United States today stem from an excess of democracy. . . . Needed, instead, is a greater degree of moderation in democracy" (Crozier, Huntington and Watanuki 1975: 113). The report defined the *excess of democracy* as when enhanced political consciousness and political participation culminate in a "deficit in governability" (Crozier, Huntington and Watanuki 1975: 173). The report stipulated that democratic input can be moderated by first balancing democracy with expert opinions, and second by limiting participation, as "the effective operation of a democratic political system usually requires some measure of apathy and noninvolvement on the part of some individuals and groups" (Crozier, Huntington and Watanuki 1975: 113–14). By controlling the expert opinions to limit the excesses of democracy, it would be easier to manufacture consent.

An important theme in this book is the consequences of the relationship between the think tank racket and journalism, insofar as they are joined together in a marriage of convenience, which benefits the former and seriously compromises the latter—which would do far more damage to both if the general public understood the extent of the "cooperation."

The notoriously close relationship between think tanks and the media corrupt the free and independent press. While it is a growing problem in print media, it is a veritable plague on television and radio. How many times have you tuned into current affairs or news programs and found a "Senior Fellow" of this, or an "analyst" from that, opining on matters of the day? Understandably, producers need guests who have expertise in the matter at hand and are suited to broadcast mediums. Let us be honest, "performing" on the box or "wireless" can be daunting and nerve-racking. Thus, it is also appealing for the media to use professional media-savvy experts for hire.

But this also irks professional journalists, who have to compete for space with folk who do not depend on publishing for a livelihood. The funding for print media has been reduced significantly, which makes it difficult for journalists to compete with the think tanks that offer capable writers for free. After all, the think tanks are getting paid much more to push a specific agenda while the poor professional journalists who have to compete with them are at least technically free from this imperative, though foreknowledge of the desired narrative undoubtedly exercises its weight. And when journalism is hollowed out, the public interest loses.

On the Russia (and broader Eastern European) beat, think tank influence is becoming increasingly dangerous and malign, leading to a crisis in journalistic standards which seemingly nobody wants to acknowledge. The Western political-media establishment has declared a de-facto war against Russia's RT, constantly accusaing it of propaganda long before full censorship was imposed in 2022.

However, RT is a news organization that does not conceal from the consumers of its content that it is state-funded and presents world news from the perspectives of Russia. State-controlled media as a communicator is less efficient in promoting state policy as it invokes skepticism and caution among the audience due to its awareness of the possibility or even likelihood of an state-directed agenda. In contrast, Western think tanks have infiltrated purportedly independent news organizations in a deliberate effort to conceal their funding and objectives. Propaganda to a large extent requires concealing one's own agenda by laundering narratives through seemingly impartial intermediaries. Propaganda also entails denigrating the sources of the competing narratives by depicting them as untrustworthy, manipulative, co-opted, and belligerent.

Spinning Serbia

An outstanding example of how the media facilitates this came in January 2019 when Vladimir Putin was making a state visit to Serbia, which is, by some distance, the most pro-Russian country west of the old Soviet Union and almost certainly also the most hostile to NATO. This is hardly a surprise, given how the U.S.-led alliance bombed it only two decades ago, during a 78-day campaign, followed by NATO countries violating international law by recognizing the independence of Kosovo in 2008, a region of Serbia.

Clearly, in this context, the vast majority of Serbian foreign policy experts would look upon Putin's visit as a broadly positive event. Despite this, one pundit kept cropping up in western media around the time of the visit who was incredibly hostile to the Russian President's presence in Belgrade: Jelena Milic, described by Germany's *Der Spiegel* as a "political scientist . . . from the Belgrade Center for Euroatlantic Studies" (Verseck 2019).

This all seemed rather bizarre because one would have to look very hard in Belgrade to find someone who preferred NATO to Russia, for reasons which should be self-explanatory. Yet, a quick search revealed that so many western outlets were pushing Milic, including the likes of the BBC, where Milic was quoted as stating that "cutting the key avenue of Russian influence in the region" was the most important objective if Serbia and NATO were to get closer (Delauney 2018).

So what is the Center for Euro-Atlantic Studies (CEAS) in Belgrade? Well, it describes itself as "an independent socio-liberal think-tank organization founded in 2007" and declares its motto to be "Progress, Determination, Influence." Where things get really interesting is when you look at who funds CEAS. A lot of these names will ring a bell, such as the National Endowment for Democracy, the European Commission, German Marshall Fund, NATO's Public Diplomacy Division, and the U.S. Embassy in Serbia. CEAS is also associated with the Atlantic Council, partnering with its "DisinfoPortal."

All this means Euronews, *Der Spiegel*, and BBC, among other outlets, have allowed Milic to opine on their platforms on NATO and Russia, without pointing out that her think tank is funded by the military alliance, which requires Russia as an enemy to justify its continued existence. To be fair to Milic, she hardly hides her efforts to lobby for NATO in her homeland. Indeed, for eight years now, she has organized Belgrade's NATO week, an event designed to promote the alliance's virtue (never mind that unfortunate NATO pounding two decades ago . . .). No matter what, you have to admire the chutzpah because going to bat for NATO in Belgrade is much the same as lobbying for a Soviet Union redux in Riga or selling portraits of Henry Kissinger in Cambodia. As an aside, the 2018 edition was "supported" by NATO's Public Diplomacy Division and the United States Embassy in Serbia.

Spinning Hungary

A case from November 2018 illustrates this perfectly. At the time, Hungary and Ukraine were embroiled in a standoff regarding the rights of ethnic Hungarians in the latter country. The disagreement was entirely local, with roots in the 20th-century carving-up of Budapest's territory after it found itself on the losing side in both World Wars. As a result, Hungarian lands were dispersed into other nations—former Czechoslovakia, Romania, Yugoslavia, and the Soviet Union.

The "Treaty of Trianon" remains a strong source of bitterness to this day. In the 1920 deal, Budapest lost an incredible two-thirds of its territory, half of its total population, and about a third of its Hungarian-speaking populace. Even today, there are deep grievances in Hungary as it concerns Trianon. In 2010, nearly a century later, the Hungarian parliament declared June 4 as "the day of national belonging," marking the date it was signed. For the next two decades, Hungarians stewed over the consequences of making the disastrous choice to ally with Nazi Germany in World War Two.

There are tensions, to varying degrees, between Hungary and pretty much all the successor states housing its lost diaspora, especially since Viktor Orban started handing out passports to compatriots stranded on foreign soil. Until the Kiev "Maidan" which installed a pro-American / anti-Russian government in Ukraine, in 2014, most of the focus was on disagreements with Slovakia, but after that attention switched to Ukraine.

This decision in Budapest was largely a response to the changes in Kiev, which pursued very nationalist policies after the coup. In a bid to appease "patriotic" Ukrainian fundamentalists, Kiev began moves towards restrictive language laws, which has especially alienated the small band of Hungarian speakers on its western frontier. Predictably, Budapest rushed in to defend its "people," and now we have a nasty little imbroglio with entrenched headbangers on both sides.

The tensions between Hungary and Ukraine are not about Russia. But Western media, egged on by think tank "experts," keeps banging this drum. In late 2018, the *Los Angeles Times* sent a correspondent to Uzhgorod, a Ukrainian border city. Rather than merely reporting from the ground, the writer devoted a greater part of the article to Russia, intimating that Orban is operating in lock-step with Moscow. This is laughable to anybody who understands the Hungarian Prime Minister's political methods. The article reeked of disinformation.

Who was the expert used to "back up" these assertions? Only one Peter Kreko, "director of the Political Capital Institute, a Budapest think tank," who was concerned that Orban's moves "help Russia hamper Ukraine's Euro-Atlantic integration." The *LA Times* was not transparent and didn't disclose Kreko's funding. Who bankrolls the "Political Capital Institute, a Budapest think tank": Institute of Modern Russia (plaything of disgraced former 90's oligarch and Putin opponent Mikhail Khodorkovsky)? The National Endowment For Democracy (a U.S. neoconservative outlet dedicated to "regime change" and promoting a pro-U.S. outlook in Eastern Europe, whose chair has dubbed Ukraine "the big prize"); Open Society (George Soros, who needs no introduction); Atlantic Council; European Values (a Soros-funded Prague lobby group which smeared hundreds of European public figures as "useful idiots" for appearing on RT, including Jeremy Corbyn and Stephen Fry); German Marshall Fund of the United States.

Corrupting the Media

The intimate relationship between think tanks and the media corrupt the latter. A clear example of the ethical conflict of this relationship came in October 2019, during the U.S. media hysteria over Joe Biden and Donald Trump's dealings with Ukraine. This dominated the news agenda around that time, especially given it resulted in the U.S. president facing impeachment proceedings.

GQ magazine, the men's style bible of my impressionable youth, used to also provide the odd decent political or cultural, article. However, as with most British and American media, standards have fallen dramatically in recent years, as bean counters increasingly call the shots. And journalists take more satisfaction in being liked by the Twitter masses than acting as a thorn in the side of elites. During the height of the Ukraine story, it ran a piece by Julia Ioffe (2019), a Russian-born American reporter, designed to explain "why Ukraine pops up in so many U.S. scandals."

To be fair to Ioffe, a lot of the local nuance was spot on. However, from the point of view of ethics, the report was highly questionable. Right after Ioffe discussed Burisma (the Ukrainian gas company which paid Biden's son Hunter up to $50,000 monthly to sit on its board, despite his having no qualifications or experience in the sector), she quoted two Atlantic Council lobbyists, without mentioning Burisma is one of its biggest funders.

In fact, she only told her readers that one of the pair, Daniel Fried, was connected to the pro-NATO pressure group, and failed to mention at all that the second, Evelyn Farkas, was also attached. Now, this is a big deal. It's part of a pattern of conflict of interest—whether lazy or deliberate—which makes a mockery of the objectivity journalists ought to uphold. Additionally, it dupes the reader, who will likely believe commentators chosen by a given reporter are genuine impartial experts.

How, in the name of all that's reasonable, could two people employed by an organization bankrolled by Burisma be judged suitable to comment on a story directly involving the Kiev gas giant? Of course, this pattern of behavior is not restricted to matters directly concerning the United States. For example, in Ireland, the *Irish Times* is the establishment bible and has long been regarded as the "paper of record." Back in March 2018, one Edward Burke published an op-ed rubbishing Ireland's traditional military neutrality and lauding Dublin authorities for expelling a Russian diplomat. This was around the time of the Skripal case, when Sergei, a Russian-born British spy, and his daughter Julia, were poisoned in Salisbury, allegedly at the hands of the Russians.

In his piece, Burke assailed Mary Lou McDonald, the de facto opposition leader (the second largest Irish party, Fianna Fail was then propping up the Fine Gael government in a "confidence and supply" arrangement), who had expressed skepticism over Britain's version of the events surrounding the case. Burke also directed fire at her British counterpart, Jeremy Corbyn, for not fully swallowing the verdict of UK national security adviser, Mark Sedwill.

The writer went on to say "Ireland and other EU member states were fully justified in expelling Russian embassy officials" while demanding Ireland "rigorously apply any future EU sanctions aimed at punishing the Putin regime." In conclusion, the *Irish Times* recorded how "Dr. Edward Burke is an assistant professor in international relations at the University of Nottingham."

The newspaper did not inform its readers that the author was, to quote his own biography, previously "a lecturer in strategic studies at the University of Portsmouth" (which trains UK military officers from RAF Cranwell). Nor did the *Irish Times* refer to his one-time role as "Strategy, Planning, Analysis and Reporting Officer at the EU Police Mission in Afghanistan." Surely this is relevant when someone is pushing the word of the UK's national security advisor as gospel and insisting Ireland must "rigorously apply" EU sanctions against Russia?

Invading the Baltic States

Another weird think tank narrative that found its way into the mainstream press is the idea of contemporary Russia conquering the Baltic states. In 2019, RAND published a 36-page report, compiled by five authors on "Deterring Russian Aggression in the Baltic States Through Resilience and Resistance" (RAND 2019b). The intent was to explain how "Estonia, Latvia, and Lithuania can deter and counteract Russian hybrid aggression and military attacks in the Baltic region." No evidence was given as to why this seemed a possibility or how Moscow would go about launching a military attack against them. In typical RAND fashion, it amounted to a pitch for military spending by the Baltic states, which benefits RAND's sponsors. "The authors estimate that a robust technology initiative to enhance these capabilities for all three states would cost about $125 million, could be implemented over several years, and is scalable," the report argued.

Then you have the Atlantic Council. "The Baltic region today is marred by dangerous brinkmanship, as Russian forces taunt U.S. and allied militaries with provocative maneuvers," a 2018 report announced. "Broad consensus now recognizes the nature of the threat from the Kremlin—no longer disputed, dismissed, downplayed." Nevertheless, the "broad consensus" was not backed up by a citation. And may well have been a figment of author Damon Wilson's imagination. And his remedy for this supposed threat? "Ensure a continuous U.S. military presence in the Baltic states" and "Invest more in our frontlines allies who invest in their own defense."

The second point basically translates as "spend more money on the Balts if they spend more on American weapons"—which, of course, benefits the outlets that bankroll the Atlantic Council. And the first one is a red flag to a bull. The two major invasions of Russia in modern history both came from its European frontier. France in the 19th century and Germany in the 20th, with around 27 million Soviet citizens killed in the latter attack. Russia remains highly sensitive to encroachment on its borders, which is why Russia seized Crimea in

2014 after the Western-backed coup in Ukraine due to the fear that the Russian Black Sea Fleet would be evicted from Sevostopol and the port later leased to NATO. The Russian invasion in February 2022 similarly was a reaction to the provocations from NATO's growing military presence in Ukraine and the prospect of NATO expansion. Yet provoking Russia becomes a source for NATO unity and arms sales. In comparison, Prussian Chancellor Otto von Bismarck provoked France to declaring war on Prussia in 1870 to incentivise the German states to unify against the French, which resulted in German unification in 1871.

That said, the Atlantic Council is merely trying to please its paymasters, which is clear from the conclusion. "We need to move beyond the current mindset in which we allocate $2 million in Foreign Military Financing and $1 million in IMET—training, and education—per Baltic nation," Wilson writes. "We could use a combination of loans and grants to support larger-scale investment in their own defense." He even lays out a plan for how and from where such funding could be secured, "Furthermore, we can use this approach to incentive joint planning and procurement among the three nations, as the U.S. Senate has already attempted to do. These funds could be drawn from, or designated within, the generous plus up of the European Deterrence Initiative."

So it is all about the money and amounted to a sales pitch. But the Russian audience did not see it that way. Atlantic Council's hysteria over Russian intentions in the Balts has been a recurring theme. Back in January 2016, Stephen Blank penned a bizarre article saying "it is likely that we would see snap exercises, plus some combination of Russia's power projection forces go into operation to seal the Baltic Sea and seize territories" (Blank 2016).

As if a future Russian invasion was essentially a given. CEPA, naturally, was equally hysterical. "In the summer of 2017, the Center for European Policy Analysis sent Colin Dueck on a listening tour of the Baltics. . . . He reports back that winter is coming and the Baltic states, as well as the United States, cannot afford to ignore their restless neighbor to the East," according to the pressure group (CEPA 2017).

"Washington should consider deploying one U.S. battalion to Lithuania, from forces already in Europe," Dueck argued. "Not only would this be most welcome in that country but by clustering U.S. forces both north and south of the Suwalki gap, Moscow would be presented with a more vivid indication that any invasion of the Baltics would mean confronting American troops."

The noise think tanks kicked up over the Baltics helped to embed the idea that a Russian invasion is some sort of inevitability. The media copied this outlook. Here is an example of how casual it could be. Gary Shteyngart, a noted American writer, who teaches at Columbia University, penned a spring 2016 piece for *Travel + Leisure*, a prestigious New York magazine that sold just under a million copies in 2012.

It was set in Kiev, Ukraine's capital. He relates a dinner encounter with Masha Gessen, a Russian-born American journalist, who previously ran U.S. state media RFE/RL's operation in Moscow, indicating how the think tank Baltic narrative has led to a sort of derangement. "Talk naturally falls to the topic du jour: which country will Putin invade next?" Gessen's glib take: "He lost in Ukraine and is losing in Syria, so Estonia's next," Shteyngart recalls.

He continues: "having put that issue to rest, we order dessert. Nostalgia triumphs and we go for the Kiev torte, a dry Soviet creation." This all feeds some sort of mainstream media assumption that a Russian attack on these countries is a given. Despite there being no evidence to support the notion Moscow has ever contemplated such action. "What If Russia Invaded the Baltics—and Donald Trump Was President?" *The Atlantic* announced hysterically in 2016.

The Open Skies Treaty

In late 2019. The Open Skies treaty suddenly became a big deal. Originally conceived back in 1955 by U.S. President Dwight Eisenhower, it received a frosty response from the Soviets and was buried for more than three decades. Then George Bush Senior dusted it off in the late 1980s. It was finally implemented in 2002.

With 34 members as of 2019, the agreement allowed unarmed aerial surveillance flights over the territory of its participants. So, Ukraine could fly over Moscow, and Americans could take a look at Vladivostok. Or Britain could jaunt around Belarus. And vice versa. The idea was to help remove mutual suspicion and distrust, and reduce the risks of war, because signatories can gather information about military activities of concern to them. Yet, even though the U.S. conducted more than twice as many surveillance flights over Russia as Russia did over American land, it is Washington that wanted to pull the plug.

All data was shared among the members, on request. And the system worked well since its inception. But then came Donald Trump. Consistent with his role as a destroyer of treaties encouraging international cooperation, he took a wrecking ball to the agreement in 2019.

Here's an October 2019 tweet from Senator James Lankford, a Republican from Oklahoma: "The U.S. should withdraw from the Open Skies Treaty. In the last 30 years technology has changed significantly and now this treaty only benefits Russia."

"Wrong. Gives U.S. unclassified imagery of Russia & allows NATO allies to conduct overflights as well. U.S./NATO have conducted many more flights over Russia than Russia over the U.S.," replied Stephen Pifer, a career diplomat, who served as the United States Ambassador to Ukraine under Bill Clinton, and as Deputy Assistant Secretary of State in the Bureau of European and Eurasian Affairs with responsibility for Russia and Ukraine in George Bush Junior's first term.

Pifer knows his stuff, and now that he was retired, he could speak his mind. And the fact is not a single neutral U.S., EU or Russian expert believed cancelation of Open Skies would benefit the security of its 34 adherents. Weakening the scheme will only increase tensions. Which, of course, benefits only those who profit from conflict. Thus, it was pretty inevitable the Think Tank racket would support Trump's initiative, given the influence of military contractors on balance sheets.

Predictably, it was not hard to find pliant media, willing to amplify the message, either. One example appeared in the *National*

Review, the conservative bible founded by the late Bill Buckley in the 1950s. The author was one Rebeccah Heinrichs, who lobbies for the Hudson Institute, a RAND spin-off, which takes in $17 million a year from its donors. It is hardly surprising that those donors include various military contractors. Northrop Grumman, Lockheed Martin, Boeing, Rivada Networks would all stand to lose if relations between Russian and the U.S. improve as it would mean a reduction in defense spending. What's more the 2018 annual report (on page 57) from the Hudson Institute featured a photo of its top brass hanging out at Lockheed's F-35 assembly facility in Fort Worth, Texas. Just in case anyone missed the association.

Naturally, the *National Review* did not enlighten its readers concerning Heinrichs' Hudson Institute connection; in fact, it, provided no bio for Heinrichs at all. Which was notable because the piece was almost entirely inaccurate. Right from the start the lede stated: "The treaty costs us [the U.S.] money that could better be spent on other aspects of national defense, and benefits us less than it benefits Russia."

"The handwringing is overdone. Whatever purpose it used to serve, the costs of the treaty to the United States now outweigh the benefits. The Trump administration should withdraw from it," she stated (Heinrichs 2019). And as for the reasons? a) Russia is not complying with the letter or spirit of the treaty b) Russia has been limiting and preventing flights over those parts of its territory in which there is the most interest among U.S. allies: Kaliningrad, Abkhazia, South Ossetia, and Chechnya and c) the United States has tried to persuade Russia to act responsibly.

Let us now bring in Steffan Watkins, an Ottawa-based open-source intelligence research consultant, and expert on Open Skies. "This is a buffet of propaganda," was his first reaction. He notes how Heinrichs cites the aforementioned Senator Cotton, who said: "(POTUS) should withdraw from the treaty and redeploy the hundreds of millions of dollars the Pentagon wastes on Open Skies flights and equipment to increase U.S. combat power."

"Buy more arms, not cameras, is the rhetoric from the Senator bankrolled by the arms industry," Watkins observed. "Heinrichs and Cotton tag team journalists giving an impression of impartiality, but between synchronized tweets, and out-of-date talking points from 2016, this article is nothing but a partisan attack on the treaty and cannot be taken seriously."

Watkins also points out that the issues go way beyond Russia and the U.S. "For the 32 states other than Russia and the U.S., they don't have crazy spy satellites, so this low-level classified imagery, that is shared across all 34 countries, is very useful, and the cameras are all tamperproof, so they know there's no funny business with tampered Satellite imagery from 'another party,'" he argued. "It's good for everyone, and arguably neutral for the U.S. It's certainly not "bad" because they don't leave the aliens out in the yard at Area 51, or whatever"

"Think of Greece vs Turkey; they can use the Open Skies Treaty to diffuse their issues, which pop up now and again," Watkins continued. "This is usually framed as a U.S./Russia thing, but there is a matrix of different countries who all use it for their own reasons." Yet, the think tank racket does not care about these concerns, because peace and harmony are bad for business.

19. Think Tanks on Covid and Russia

Back in March 2020, as the Covid-19 epidemic raged, Vladimir Putin called Italian Prime Minister Giuseppe Conte. During the conversation, Conte asked for help in fighting the coronavirus, according to the Kremlin readout which has not been contradicted by Italian officials. Contrary to perception, other European Union states did try to help the Italians. Germany and France, in particular, took patients and sent supplies, despite dealing with outbreaks of their own. However, Rome's NATO allies in the U.S. and UK were largely absent from the scene. Towards the end of the month, Russia stepped in.

Let us be clear from the outset, there was undoubtedly a strong PR, as well as practical, element to Russia's assistance. Every country in the world likes to be perceived favorably. It's worth noting that Rome has been obliged, due to EU membership, to support collective sanctions against Russia related to Moscow's reabsorption of Crimea in 2014. No doubt Moscow hoped—as pointed out by Diplomatic Editor of BBC's *Newsnight,* Mark Urban, a vocal Russia critic and hardly a Kremlin patsy—hat Italy's politicians would one day remember the helping hand. Putin was also surely thinking ahead to a post-coronavirus crisis time when Italians might remember who stood by them in their hour of need, especially given Italy was the third most powerful country in the European Union which had Russia under sanctions.

Moscow sent teams of doctors, protective gear, and medical equipment to the Covid-stricken country. The detail included 100 military virologists and epidemiologists, along with eight medical teams, according to Russian news outlets. Most importantly, it delivered 600 ventilators. This was a significant amount, given Italy apparently had only about 5,000 of the devices. Indeed, a few days after the Putin/Conte call, *The New York Times* was writing about Italy's "ventilator crisis."

While Moscow desired some positive publicity, the unofficial job description of think tanks is also to deny Russia positive coverage. A few days after the aid landed, a campaign began to discredit the Russian initiative. One of the first tweets came from Oliver Carroll, of London's *Independent* newspaper. "Some Italians are expressing unease about Putin's Covid-19 emergency aid," he wrote. "According to *La Stampa*, 80 percent of supplies are 'useless,' and sources worry about high-ranking military officers now in the country. Russian soldiers are free to roam in Italy a few steps away from NATO," the paper warned. "*La Stampa* says China sent masks [and] ventilators; Russia sent irrelevant equipment used for bacteriological and chemical outbreaks." Carroll added, "[There is a] belief that Russia . . . [is] not helping us only for great goodness of its people... now beginning to circulate in broad sectors, military and political."

The newspaper's report seemingly relied on the testimony of an anonymous source, who did not give their name. Thus, we have to take the author's word for it. However, the same day, Italy's Ambassador to Moscow had a rather different point-of-view. "Pasquale Terracciano thanked Russia for its assistance in the fight against novel coronavirus, adding that the humanitarian aid to his country included about 600 medical ventilators," reported the TASS news agency. It then quoted Terracciano as saying "it is very important that all this medical equipment includes 600 ventilators, which are critically important at this stage of the epidemic."

Meanwhile, the president of Lombardy, the Italian region most affected by the Covid-19 crisis, openly dismissed *La Stampa*'s report. "I say thanks to the Russians who sent us doctors and other people who can help with disinfection," Attilio Fontana told an online press conference. "The Russian Federation has sent face masks, ventilators, and medical staff and teams to disinfect public buildings and our cities," Italian Foreign Minister Di Maio said. "They have helped in their own way in an act of solidarity."

Those entitled to speak for Italy seemed to be pretty grateful for Moscow's aid. Nevertheless, predictably, the "Atlanticists" were not happy. After all, a Europe without confrontational dividing lines puts an end to the demand for U.S. leadership. When Gorbachev was working to end the Cold War, similar hawks in Washington warned against the "peace offensive," as reduced fear of the Soviets would weaken the foundation of the Western alliance.

Eto Buziashvili of the Atlantic Council wrote on Twitter that "80% of the Covid-19 supplies that Russia has sent to Italy are useless," citing *La Stampa*. Her Twitter biography, by the way, claims she is an expert in "disinformation." Next up was Olga Tokariuk, who writes for Atlantic Council as well as a Kiev-based news site, Hromadske, which is bankrolled by the local U.S. embassy. "According to *La Stampa* sources in the Italian military, 80% of items they [the Russians] brought are useless," she tweeted. "Italy recently reported that 80% of Russian aid against #Covid_19 is useless," wrote Dionis Cenusa. He also pens articles for, you guessed it, the Atlantic Council. Also, note that he says "Italy recently reported," not *La Stampa*.

One of the Atlantic Council's more high-profile lobbyists, Michael Weiss, also joined in. The "fellow" noted how "80% of Russian coronavirus aid to Italy is useless, apparently." What is most interesting here is the fact that so many of the people pushing the disinformation panning the Russian contribution are connected to the pro-NATO pressure group—not to mention the fact that they addressed it in almost the same terms. Was this coordination, or coincidence?

Circling back to the original *La Stampa* piece, it seemed logical to check whether the reporter had any think tank links himself. Not surprisingly, it turns out Jacopo Iacoboni has also written for the Atlantic Council. He most notably assisted Alina Polyakova with a 2017 report dubbed "The Kremlin's Trojan Horses." This hit job smeared numerous Italian public figures — such as politicians Beppe

Grillo and Matteo Salvini—as effectively operating as proxies for Moscow. Polyakova has since been appointed to run CEPA.

It turns out Iacoboni's anti-Russia credentials are quite well known. Indeed, he has even been endorsed by the Integrity Initiative, the above-mentioned British government-funded undercover "information warrior." This is not to imply Iacoboni knew he was being considered by the British for their operations, but it does mean they regarded him as reliably anti-Russian. Which tells its own tale.

The *La Stampa* story, based on anonymous sources which may or may not be legitimate, was a curious intervention at a time when Italy was on its knees. It is quite instructive that the think tank crowd, most notably those from the Atlantic Council who rarely show any interest in Italian affairs, jumped on it. As is the author's own association with the pro-NATO institution. Make of it what you will.

Russia's efforts to fight Covid-19 were denounced as propaganda. Moscow's delivery of masks, protective gear, ventilators, and medical teams to Italy, was framed as a sinister ploy to create political goodwill to improve relations and weaken Italy's support for anti-Russian sanctions. *Forbes* Magazine quoted Natalie Tocci, the director of the most prominent Italian think tank, Institute for International Affairs, who argued that Russian aid to Italy is aimed to undermine the EU: "Russia needs a quick win.... It does what Russia always does, which is seize low-hanging fruit" (Togoh 2020).

Saving Italian lives when the other Europeans did not was portrayed as an evil design to undermine the EU. These allegations were also repeated by *The Wall Street Journal*, which quoted General Vincenzo Camporini, former chief of staff of the Italian armed forces, who warned against Russia's nefarious attempt at portraying itself as a friend to Italy: "It's very unpleasant that our tragedy is being exploited for propaganda purposes" (Trofimov 2020). General Camporini happens to be vice president of the same Italian think tank, the Institute for International Affairs. In the Western media, the Institute for International Affairs seemingly served as the official representative of Italians.

Predictably, the BBC also ran with the story of the malign Russian Covid assistance but took a somewhat different approach. Insofar as Russia sent military virologists, British state media deemed it a military mission. The BBC (2020) warned that "a Russian military mission had been allowed to operate within 50km (30 miles) of a U.S. military base in a NATO member state."

CEPA Weighs In on Covid-19

In April 2020, CEPA held a "Virtual Event" about Russia's Covid-19 Moment. The event's host was Polyakova, CEPA's president. She had posted a factually incorrect tweet a week before the event, alleging that Russia had sent "mostly useless and malfunctioning supplies" to Italy to help with its coronavirus crisis. The same trope was pushed by her ex-colleagues at the Atlantic Council.

The host insisted that Russia was concealing its infection numbers and comparing the gravity to Chernobyl. Moscow's deliveries of supplies to Italy and the U.S. were dismissed as having "large propaganda value," although it was not clear why there had not been similar complaints about the Russian gear flown to New York if 80% of the Russian equipment was "useless." The Russian newsnetwork RT was also a topic for the Covid debate as it was suggested RT ran an article saying Covid-19 was a U.S.-made SARS-like "bio weapon" based on comments from Philip Giraldi, an ex-CIA officer. What RT (2020) actually had reported was that Hossein Salami, head of Iran's elite Revolutionary Guards said this. RT's article did not endorse Salami's theory, nor did it cite Giraldi, it merely outlined the facts of what was said. Iran's Press TV—which has nothing to do with RT—used a statement from Giraldi in its coverage.

Another topic related to Covid was the wishful thinking about the reduced stability of "the regime" in Russia as a result of the pandemic. It is worth mentioning the first rule of Russia punditry or journalism: If an analyst describes the Russian government as "the regime," their output is riddled with biases. Anyway, it is implied that Russia puts a lower value on "human suffering" than the U.S. (tell that to the people of Iraq, and various other places). It is also speculated that there is a risk for Moscow if technocrats and regional governors handle the pandemic too well, as it could set a precedent and make it harder for the Kremlin to further centralize power.

20. Think Tanks and the Information War in Ukraine

The war in Ukraine has driven global military spending to new levels as the distinction between a direct war and proxy war between NATO and Russia becomes increasingly obscured. This development results in more money available for think tanks, which are tasked with shaping the media narrative and policies. The think tanks have become interwoven into the Military-Industrial Complex to such an extent that former CIA analyst Ray McGovern has developed a more fitting term: The Military-Industrial-Congressional-Intelligence-Media-Academia-Think-Tank complex (MICIMATT), which is pushing the world closer to nuclear war.

The U.S. overshadowed all other states by spending $877 billion in 2022, making up 39 percent of total global military spending (Sipri 2023). With the U.S. and its allies emptying their weapons storages to keep the Ukrainian proxy war going, business is better than ever for the military-industrial complex. As a result, there is plenty of funding available for the think tanks to shape the elite discussions and policies concerning the war. In May 2023, Responsible Statecraft reported that the think tank Council on Foreign Relations (CFR) was considering James Taiclet for its board of directors. Taiclet is the chairman and CEO of Lockheed Martin, making him the world's largest arms dealer (Clifton 2023).

Once again, the think tanks are wielding significant influence as they produce reports for policymakers, shape the media landscape with their op-eds, and provide employment for politicians out of office. The think tankers also have a strong presence in the Biden administration, which unavoidably will influence policies.

While it is difficult to measure the extent to which the think tanks have influenced policies and the media narrative, it is worth exploring the key role of think tanks and the skewed narratives disseminated about the Ukrainian war to which they contributed. A study by FAIR, a media watchdog group, reveals that the experts from hawkish think tanks funded by the weapons industry were overwhelmingly overrepresented in the media (Kempthorne 2022).

Shaping the Narrative

Information warfare is a key part of any armed conflict, which makes think tanks an indispensable instrument of power. As the Chinese military strategist Sun Tzu said, "all warfare is based on deception." During the Second World War, Churchill famously stated: "In wartime, truth is so precious that she should always be attended by a bodyguard of lies." Similarly, in the words of Walter Lippman: "We must remember that in time of war what is said on the enemy's side of the front is always propaganda, and what is said on our side of the front is truth and righteousness, the cause of humanity and a crusade for peace."

Since Russia invaded in February 2022, the Institute for the Study of War (ISW) has become the media's go-to think tank for updates and analysis. The lack of objectivity of the Institute for the Study of War has previously been reported. The founder and president of the Institute of War is Kimberly Kagan, working there with her husband Fredrick Kagan, who according to *The Washington Post* in 2012 both developed close ties with General Petraeus and helped "to shore up support for the [Afghanistan] war among Republican leaders on Capitol Hill" (Chandrasekaran 2012). Frederick Kagan is the brother of Robert Kagan, who was a founder of the Project for a New American Century (PNAC), which had a central role in the Bush administration and the decision to invade Iraq. Furthermore, Robert Kagan's wife is Victoria Nuland, the U.S. Under Secretary of State for Political Affairs who had a key role in the Western-backed coup in Kiev in 2014. The ISW sent a clear message that the road to peace is merely to produce more weapons and to send these weapons to the frontline: "The balance of overall available resources and industrial capacity is decisively weighted toward the West. Russian military industrial potential is, in fact, hopelessly outmatched by Western military industrial potential" (ISW 2023). Hence, the Institute for the Study of War can be considered a key actor in the U.S. disinformation war.

The discourse in most of the think tanks does not reflect any search for a path forward to successful negotiations and a political settlement for the war in Ukraine, rather the reports appear designed to shape the war narrative. This pro-war orientation undermines the ability of think tanks to produce objective analysis and play a constructive role toward promoting mutual understanding and peace—were this to be their intent. As argued by Walter Lippman, one of the groundbreaking U.S. scholars on political propaganda, the effort of portraying conflicts as a struggle between good and evil is imperative to mobilise the public but it obstructs pursuing a workable peace. To overcome the public's aversion towards conflict and war "the enemy had to be portrayed as evil incarnate, as absolute and congenital wickedness.... As a result of this impassioned nonsense, public opinion became so envenomed that the people would not countenance a workable peace" (Lippman 1955: 21).

The West's information war with regard to Ukraine has replaced any objective analysis with what can only be described as war propaganda. A key feature of propaganda is to reinvent the language to either grant or deny legitimacy to the actors involved. The think tanks repeatedly present the conflict to be between "Putin" and the "international community." Russia and its national security interest are thus delegitimized and demoted to be represented merely by "Putin" as a rogue leader. Meanwhile, the "international community" actually represents fewer than 15 percent of the world population who live in countries that have imposed sanctions on Russia and send weapons to Ukraine.

The continuously repeated and uncontested narrative of an unprovoked invasion by Putin, who is represented as the embodiment of evil, serves to make victory the only acceptable response. Repeatedly describing the invasion as "unprovoked" is imperative as it seeks to relieve NATO of any blame and to also reject any compromise. Acceptable discussions of Russian motivations have thus been limited to Russia's purported opportunistic territorial ambitions, its desire to restore the Soviet Union and "Russian imperialism," while NATO's motivations are presented as solely to defend Ukrainian freedom and democracy. All subsequent analysis must thus fit within these parameters, making the narrative a struggle between good and evil, and implying that peace can only be achieved through victory as compromise is dangerous appeasement. The continuous historical references to the Munich appeasement and Putin as the new Hitler also serve the important purpose of making negotiations and compromise dirty words, while war becomes virtuous.

Reports on the war by the ISW and most Western think tanks were shaped by the usual features of war propaganda: We did not want the war and the enemy is solely responsible for it. We are fighting for a good cause and the enemy's leader is evil. The enemy is hopelessly incompetent but compensates with sheer brutality. Our side is competent and brave but restrained by principles. Our casualties are minor and those of the enemy are large. Our war crimes are accidental, and the enemy's war crimes are deliberate and of immense scope. The conflict is between good and evil, and questioning that orientation is treasonous.

Repeating rather than contesting absurd narratives became a purity test for media and politicians alike to prove loyalty to Ukraine and the West. A few days into the Russian invasion of Ukraine, a story emerged about the "Ghost of Kiev," a Ukrainian fighter pilot who shot down approximately 40 Russian fighter jets. The story was obviously fake, yet repeating a ridiculous story became an even greater display of virtue and commitment to "our side." Another false story was the martyrdom of Ukrainian border guards on Snake Island who were asked to surrender by the Russian navy. The Ukrainian border guards responded bravely, saying "Russian warships, go to hell" before they were all killed by the Russian navy. While the martyrs were celebrated across all Western media channels, if one could change to Russian TV one would see all the soldiers who were being interviewed after surrendering. However, given the censorship of Russian media in the West, this was not an option in many countries. Both stories were confirmed to be fake (Thompson and Alba 2022). Think tanks and most of the major newspapers in the U.S. and UK also collectively referred to Ukraine's defeat and surrender of Mariupol as an "evacuation," a creative use of language as the Ukrainian soldiers were evacuated to Russian captivity.

Russia has also been repeatedly accused of attacking the Zaporizhzhia nuclear power plant in Ukraine, despite it being under Russian control. The Russia shelling of a facility it already controlled was allegedly meant to "send a message" to the West, although Russia never bombed any of the nuclear power plants under Ukrainian control, and what the purported message could be remained incomprehensible.

Thereafter, Russia was accused of attacking and destroying the Nord Stream gas pipelines, of which it owned a 51% share. Yet again, Russia's destruction of pipelines which for it were a source of revenue and influence in Europe was portrayed as intending to send a message to the West. Perhaps, had Russia intended to send such a message, it might instead have attacked the rival Norwegian gas pipelines. Seymour Hersh published an article in which he referred to a source that confirmed the U.S., aided by Norway, had carried out the attack on the pipelines. However, the content of that report was dismissed by Western journalists who, instead of following up on the research, began to discredit Hersh. Overnight, the world's leading investigative journalist was transformed into a senile Putinist.

Russia was also accused of attacking the Kremlin with drones, which yet again think tanks insisted could only be explained as a Russian false flag operation. The continuous reference to the "Russian playbook" assisted in plugging the absence of logic in Western narratives. While these disinformation narratives were an affront to common sense, the West's media bullhorn armed by experts from the think tanks was such that the insouciant public seems to have bought them.

Strict narrative control has been ensured by censoring Russian media across the West and shaming those in the Western media who provided a platform to Russians. Furthermore, Western journalists or academics seeking to explain the actual Russian motivations and policies were easily dismissed as Russian propagandists or useful idiots of Putin, ensuring that these journalists and academics would be denied a future platform. Michael McFaul, the former U.S. ambassador to Russia and a Senior Fellow at the Hoover Institution, even tweeted that evil had to be censored: "Please don't give Putin propagandists a platform on your media platforms. There is a time and place for hearing two sides of an issue. This tragic moment in European history is not one of them. Do not give false equivalency to voices of evil and voices of good."

The construction and management of the narrative has focused on "supporting Ukraine" in a struggle between democracy and authoritarianism, insisting that the Russian invasion was "unprovoked," and that the only acceptable outcome is a military victory.

"Supporting Ukraine": Democracy vs. Authoritarianism

The heuristics of democracy versus authoritarianism have become the contemporary script of good versus evil, providing simplistic and powerful mental shortcuts for the public to interpret all the complexities in the world. As a result, a powerful narrative has emerged that is largely immune to facts.

The foundation of any war propaganda is to assign the roles of villain, victim, and savior. Despite the assignation of these roles wherein victimized Ukraine is seeking to escape the imperial clutches of Russia, enabling NATO to play the role of the selfless and gallant savior, every poll from 1991 to 2014 demonstrated that only a small minority of Ukrainians, approximately 17%-25%, desired NATO membership. In fact, NATO warned in 2011 that its relationship with Ukraine was obstructed by the Ukrainian people: "The greatest challenge for Ukrainian-NATO relations lies in the perception of NATO among the Ukrainian people. NATO membership is not widely supported in the country, with some polls suggesting that popular support of it is less than 20%" (NATO 2011: 11).

In 2014, the West responded to the disinterest of Ukrainians in NATO by regime change. The EU initiated the destabilization of Ukraine with the proposed EU-Ukraine Association Agreement of November 2013. The agreement required Ukraine to adopt EU legislation, which would prevent Ukraine from joining the Russian-led Customs Union. The Association Agreement also included security cooperation that could be interpreted as a stepping-stone towards NATO membership, as Kiev would commit itself to "gradual convergence in the area of foreign and security policy, including the Common Security and Defence Policy" (European Union 2013). When Kiev rejected the EU agreement, both the EU and the U.S. incited and supported an uprising by the opposition which, to gain legitimacy, was sold to the public as a "democratic revolution," despite the fact that the existing Ukrainian president had been elected in a free and fair election.

The removal of Viktor Yanukovich from power was in clear violation of the Ukrainian constitution. The Maidan protests that removed him from power did not enjoy democratic majority support in Ukraine and even fewer supported a coup (BBC 2014b). A *New York Times* report repudiated the narrative of a democratic revolution: "In 2014 the United States backed an uprising—in its final stages a violent uprising—against the legitimately elected Ukrainian government of Viktor Yanukovych, which was pro-Russian" (Caldwell 2022).

Victoria Nuland, then U.S. Assistant Secretary of State for European and Eurasian affairs, admitted during the Maidan riots in December 2013 that the U.S. had invested more than $5 billion to assist Ukraine in achieving "the future it deserves" (Mearsheimer 2014: 80). U.S. Senator John McCain similarly explained what he was doing in Kiev during the protests in Kiev: "What we're trying to do is try to bring about a peaceful transition here" (*Guardian* 2013). The U.S. claimed it was working with both sides in Ukraine to reach a peaceful solution, although a leaked phone call between Victoria Nuland and Geoffrey Pyatt, the U.S. Ambassador to Ukraine, revealed a plot to topple the Ukrainian government. The phone call, leaked two weeks before the coup, discussed making Arseny Yatsenyuk the Prime Minister and other details of the makeup of the future post-coup government. Nuland also outlined how the UN could be used to legitimize the process and "glue this thing together" (BBC 2014a). Carpenter (2017) referred to the U.S. meddling as "breathtaking" insofar as Nuland and Pyatt were caught deciding who should be in the new Ukrainian government and who should be kept out, at a time when Yanukovich was still the lawful president of Ukraine. The toppling of Yanukovich by Washington was referred to it as "the most overt coup d'état in history" by George Friedman (2014), the CEO of Stratfor, also known as a "shadow CIA."

The new Ukraine was largely cleansed of the political, economic, and cultural influence of Russia, which also entailed marginalizing Ukrainians that were deemed too "Russified" or Russian-friendly. The day after President Yanukovich fled, the first act of the new Ukrainian parliament was to vote in favor of abolishing the languages of minorities, which entailed removing Russian as the second language in the south and the east of Ukraine. Michael McFaul (2021), a fellow at the Hoover Institution and the former U.S. ambassador to Moscow, later celebrated President Zelensky's crackdown on opposition politicians and media: "His decision to ban pro-Russia television networks, and to charge their owner and Putin ally Viktor Medvedchuk with treason, was a daring act that needs U.S. support."

The uprising in Donbas, protesting the Western-backed regime change in Kiev, was met with a military response. The NATO-backed government in Kiev launched an "anti-terrorist operation" against Donbas, which eventually resulted in the death of 14.000 Ukrainians. Yet, a weak Ukrainian military that was not eager to use military force against its own population was not up to the task. Thus, the right-wing nationalists, who had accrued much power during the process of regime change, subsequently developed their own far-right militia army, coming from Western Ukraine. Think tank "experts" were thus instrumental in delegitimizing Donbas fighters as mere stooges of Putin, while the right-wing ethno-nationalists were whitewashed.

One of the Nazi battalions took the name Azov Battalion after seizing control over Mariupol on the coast of the Sea of Azov, it later grew to become the Azov Regiment. Its official emblem is the Wolfsangel in front of the Black Sun, both symbols used by Nazi Germany. By 2020, the paramilitary militias in Ukraine amounted to 102,000 men, accounting for 40 percent of the entire Ukrainian armed forces (Dutta, Granados, and Ovaska 2022). These paramilitary organizations were heavily infused with nationalists from Western Ukraine, and armed and trained by Western powers.

The U.S. Congress had recognised the Azov Battalion as a Nazi organization and subsequently banned U.S. military assistance to the group in 2015 (Parry 2015b). The following year, in 2016, the U.S. Congress removed the ban on funding Nazis in Ukraine (Carden 2016). The nationalists and Western power gained significant influence over the political structures in Kiev and effectively acquired a veto over any rapprochement and peace with Donbas and Russia. The Combating Terrorism Center at West Point, the prestigious U.S. military academy, published an analysis of how the rising fascist group in Ukraine collaborated with right-wing extremists in the U.S. The report also recognized that the fascists were fiercely opposed to any peaceful settlement that entailed concessions:

> These groups have bitterly opposed any suggestion of compromise with Russia over Donbas through the Normandy negotiating process and were prominent at another rally witnessed by the author in Kyiv in the fall of 2019 to oppose concessions floated by President Volodymyr Zelensky (Lister 2020: 30).

In April 2019, Ukrainians finally had a choice to vote again on the direction of their country. Volodymyr Zelensky ran on a peace platform favoring establishing talks with Donbas, restoring normal relations with Russia, and implementing the Minsk-2 peace agreement.

Following his landslide election victory with 73 percent of the votes, Zelensky declared his intentions: "I think that we will have personnel changes. In any case we will continue in the direction of the Minsk [peace] talks and head towards concluding a ceasefire" (BBC 2019b).

But the nationalists and the U.S. were against any peaceful settlement with Donbas or Russia. On 6 October 2019, approximately 10,000 people rallied in Kiev to oppose President Zelensky's plan to end the war, which was denounced as "capitulation" (Korniienko 2019). Following the reluctance of Ukrainian troops on the front lines to pull back in accordance with the disengagement plan, Zelensky responded on 26 October 2019 by visiting the region. Upon Zelensky's arrival, the Ukrainian troops on the front-line city of Zolote openly rejected his orders to remove weapons stationed there, and one of the soldiers warned or threatened protests if these orders would be carried out. The encounter was filmed and the video spread across the internet, which revealed that President Zelensky had limited power as he could do nothing but complain: "I'm the president of this country. I'm 41 years old. I'm not a loser. I came to you and told you: remove the weapons" (Grytsenko 2019).

Andriy Biletsky, the head of National Corps and the Azov Battalion, threatened President Zelensky that if he tried to remove the soldiers from the front line then they would march on the town and "there will be thousands there instead of several dozen" (Grytsenko 2019). Sofia Fedyna, a Ukrainian lawmaker, seemingly threatened the life of Zelensky as she stated: "Mr. President thinks he is immortal... A grenade may explode there, by chance. And it would be the nicest if this happened during Moscow's shelling when someone comes to the front line wearing a white or blue shirt" (Grytsenko 2019).

An even more direct death threat came from Dmitri Yarosh, the leader of Right Sector, a far-right extremist group. Yarosh warned in May 2019, shortly after Zelensky's election victory, that fulfilling his campaign promises would have dire consequences: "He will be hanged from a tree on [Khreshchatyk Avenue], if he betrays Ukraine and the people who died during the Revolution and the War. And it is very important that he understands this" (Baud 2022).

Russia scholar Stephen Cohen argued in 2019 that Zelensky ran as a peace candidate and won an incredible peace mandate, but that the ability to deal directly with Putin was extremely challenging due to Zelensky's ultra-nationalist opponents: "they have said that they will remove and kill Zelensky if he continues along this line of negotiating with Putin." The U.S. thus had a veto over Kiev as Zelensky could not negotiate with Moscow "unless America has his back." Cohen recognized thus that "unless the White House encourages this diplomacy, Zelensky has no chance of negotiating an end to the war, so the stakes are enormously high" (Maté 2019). Washington did not offer support for Zelensky's peace mandate; this pressured Kiev to return to a confrontational stance.

After failing to assert control over the far-right groups in the military, Zelensky began to align himself closer with them (Melanovski 2021). Dmitri Yarosh, who had threatened his life in May 2019, was promoted in November 2021 to become the advisor to the Commander-in-Chief of the Ukrainian Armed Forces, while simultaneously being the head of the "Ukrainian Volunteer Army." After failing to implement his peace mandate, Zelensky's approval ratings began to falter. A poll from the Kyiv International Institute of Sociology in October 2021 revealed that Zelensky's approval had been reduced to merely 24 percent (KIIS 2021). Zelensky faced a dilemma where he would either lose his public support and peace or possibly his life, given the ire of the far-right nationalist groups. This perhaps explains the anomaly of a Jewish president leading a Nazi-influenced regime—which the West explained away by denying the existence of the Nazi elements.

During the entire buildup to the war, the effort to support the nationalists ignored the democratic will of the Ukrainian people. The war was sold as "supporting Ukraine" rather than converting the country into a Western frontline against Russia.

The "Unprovoked" Invasion

When Russia invaded, President Biden immediately presented the script about an unprovoked war, asserting: "This was never about genuine security concerns on their part. It was always about naked aggression, about Putin's desire for empire by any means necessary" (White House 2022). EU foreign policy chief Josep Borrell asserted that "'the war will have to be decided on the battlefield," while NATO Secretary General Jens Stoltenberg would later assert that "weapons are the way to peace."

Denying that NATO expansion—which had been promoted vigorously by the think tanks—had provoked the Russian invasion was imperative to deny any legitimacy to Russia's actions and to eliminate the possibility of compromise. This, despite President Bill Clinton's warning back in January 1994 that NATO expansion could redivide the continent as it could "draw a new line between East and West that could create a self-fulfilling prophecy of future confrontation" (Clinton 1994). William Perry, the former U.S. defense secretary between 1994 and 1997, had previously admitted that "in the early years [after the Cold War] I have to say that the United States deserves much of the blame" for the deteriorating relations with Russia (Borger 2016). Perry added that his colleagues in the Clinton administration recognized that NATO expansion would create conflict with Moscow, although the prevailing sentiment was that it did not matter as Russia was weak and was continuing to get weaker. Perry argued:

> It wasn't that we listened to their [Russia's] argument and said we don't agree with that argument. . . . Basically the people I was arguing with when I tried to put the Russian point ... the response that I got was really: "Who cares what they think? They're a third-rate power." And of course that point of view got across to the Russians as well. That was when we started sliding down that path (Borger 2016).

Even Joe Biden had predicted in a speech at the Atlantic Council in 1997 that NATO expansion would cause a "vigorous and hostile" response from Russia, yet Biden mocked Russia's concerns as irrelevant, as Russia would have to adjust since it did not have any other partners (Kaonga 2022). The former U.S. ambassador to Moscow, William Burns, who later became the director of the CIA, warned in a memo in 2008 that threatening to expand NATO to Ukraine could provoke a civil war and a subsequent Russian military intervention which Russia did not want to undertake:

> Not only does Russia perceive encirclement, and efforts to undermine Russia's influence in the region, but it also fears unpredictable and uncontrolled consequences which would seriously affect Russian security interests. . . . Russia is particularly worried that the strong divisions in Ukraine over NATO membership, with much of the ethnic-Russian community against membership, could lead to a major split, involving violence or at worst, civil war. In that eventuality, Russia would have to decide whether to intervene; a decision Russia does not want to have to face (Burns 2008).

In November 2021, Ukraine appeared to become a de facto NATO member as Washington and Kiev signed the "Charter on Strategic Partnership" that committed the U.S. to develop the Ukrainian army and deepen cooperation in the Black Sea, while affirming an "unwavering commitment" to reintegrate Crimea into Ukraine. Henri Guaino, a top adviser to former president Nicolas Sarkozy, warned that the charter "convinced Russia that it must attack or be attacked" (Caldwell 2022). In December 2021, the former head of Russia analysis at the CIA, George Beebe, cautioned that Russia could invade, as the U.S. was providing Ukraine with vast amounts of military equipment, training its army, and even upgrading Ukraine's Black Sea ports to fit U.S. warships. As Beebe argued: "That relationship [U.S.-Ukraine] will be far stronger and deeper, and the United States military will be more firmly entrenched inside Ukraine two to three years from now. So inaction on [the Kremlin's] part is risky" (RFE/RL 2021b).

The Proxy War Objectives

The next stage in the narrative was to insist that Russia could not be negotiated with and the only path to peace was therefore military victory. There is ample evidence suggesting that Moscow's main objective was to stop NATO expansion, which it regarded as an existential security threat, and that Moscow was prepared to make compromises to achieve this objective. Yet, the incessant Western war narrative has been that Russia cannot be negotiated with and that NATO expansion was not its motivation. This all-or-nothing narrative of resolving the conflict on the battlefield has been presented as the only acceptable outcome—one the West may come to rue.

President Obama had been cautious not to arm the anti-Russian government in Kiev as this was deemed too provocative, insofar as that military power could be used to attack Russia in Crimea, thus sparking the threat of a wider war. Yet, key think tanks cooperated to push for the militarisation of Ukraine, irrespective of it possibly provoking a war. A report jointly produced in 2015 by the Atlantic Council and Brookings Institution, the Center for a New American Security, and the Chicago Council on Global Affairs, advocated arming Ukraine with weaponry such as the Javelin anti-tank missiles. The Atlantic Council has been funded by Raytheon and Lockheed Martin, two manufacturers of the Javelin missiles. Kurt Volker, a fellow at both the Atlantic Council and CEPA, who was also a former U.S. Ambassador to NATO and a former U.S. Special Representative for Ukraine Negotiations, famously warned Biden in 2021 to oppose any reconciliation with Russia to avoid war, as the route to "success is confrontation" (Volker 2021). Volker was also an executive director of the McCain Institute, whose financial backers included the BGR Group, a lobbyist for the Javelin-producing Raytheon.

The Atlantic Council has taken a leading role in influencing U.S. policy to arm Ukraine. Known as the think tank of NATO, its board features no fewer than four previous directors of the CIA: James Woolsey, Leon Panetta, Robert Gates, and David Petraeus. The Atlantic Council has also hosted Joe Biden on several occasions, which the Atlantic Council (2016) identified as "the point person on Ukraine in the Obama administration."

In a speech hosted by the Atlantic Council in 2014, Biden advocated for European diversification away from Russian natural gas (Atlantic Council 2014). Towards this end, the Atlantic Council envisioned a key role for Burisma, the Ukrainian gas company on whose board Hunter Biden was hired with a generous salary, despite having no background in either the gas industry or Ukraine. In 2017, the Atlantic Council and Burisma signed a cooperative agreement, with a focus on "energy security." Needless to say, the Atlantic Council has a strong interest in adavocating the militarization of Ukraine-Russia relations and avoiding any rapprochement. Michael Carpenter, a key advisor of Joe Biden, is also a fellow at the Atlantic Council and a renowned supporter of Ukraine's most hawkish posture toward Russia.

The 2015 report by the Atlantic Council suggests concerns that arming Ukraine will provoke a war are unfounded as "President Poroshenko has said there can be no military solution and has sought a negotiated settlement" (Atlantic Council 2015: 3). Yet, arming Ukraine and not implementing the peace agreement meant that a military solution became an increasingly likely solution to the conflict.

The peace agreement of February 2015—the Minsk-2 peace treaty with full standing in international law—was acceptable to Moscow as it provided Donbas with autonomous rights to preserve the Russian language and resist NATO expansion. However, rather than pressure Kiev to honor its obligations, the West sabotaged the Minsk initiative for 7 years to use the delay to build a powerful Ukrainian army. After Russia invaded in 2022, it was revealed that neither Germany nor France had any intention of seeing the Minsk-2 agreement implemented, despite having negotiated purportedly to serve as its guarantors. As admitted by Angela Merkel, the Minsk Agreement was an initiative to buy time for building up the Ukrainian army: It was "an attempt to give Ukraine time" and it worked as "[Ukraine] used this time to get stronger, as you can see today" (Hildrebrandt and di Lorenzo 2022). Her French counterpart, François Hollande, confirmed: "Yes, Angela Merkel is right on this point" and "There will only be a way out of the conflict when Russia fails on the ground" (Prouvost 2022). The decision to undermine the Minsk peace agreement made war more likely as all sides had reiterated for seven years that it was the agreement was the only peaceful path to end the conflict in Ukraine while providing for its integrity.

Russia's decision to invade Ukraine appeared to follow the Clausewitzian concept of war as an extension of politics, in which Russia would impose a settlement on Ukraine that had been undermined by the West since the coup of 2014. Within the first days of the Russian invasion, Moscow and Kiev entered negotiations. The two sides were close to a peace agreement that would involve Russia pulling its troops out of Ukraine in return for Ukraine guaranteeing it would not join NATO. This proved that peace with Russia could be reached, and that its main objective was to end NATO expansion toward its borders.

This tentative peace agreement was confirmed by Fiona Hill, a former official at the U.S. National Security Council, and Angela Stent, a former National Intelligence Officer for Russia and Eurasia:

> According to multiple former senior U.S. officials we spoke with, in April 2022, Russian and Ukrainian negotiators appeared to have tentatively agreed on the outlines of a negotiated interim settlement: Russia would withdraw to its position on February 23, when it controlled part of the Donbas region and all of Crimea, and in exchange, Ukraine would promise not to seek NATO membership and instead receive security guarantees from a number of countries (Hill and Stent 2022).

Yet, the negotiations abruptly came to an end after a visit to Kiev by British Prime Minister Boris Johnson. Former Israeli Prime Minister Naftali Bennett, who led the peace negotiations, confirmed that both Moscow and Kiev had made significant compromises and "both sides very much wanted a ceasefire." However, the West "blocked" the peace agreement as there was a "decision by the West to keep striking Putin" instead of pursuing peace. According to Bennett: "there was a good chance of reaching a ceasefire, had they [the West] not curbed it" (Semonsen 2023). Turkey, which also made an effort to mediate peace, likewise confirmed the West's unwillingness to pursue peace. Turkish Foreign Minister Mevlut Cavusoglu asserted that some NATO countries aimed to extend the war to bleed and weaken Russia:

> After the talks in Istanbul, we did not think that the war would take this long . . . But following the NATO foreign ministers' meeting, I had the impression that there are those within the NATO member states that want the war to continue—let the war continue and Russia gets weaker. They don't care much about the situation in Ukraine (Semonsen 2023).

Retired German General Harald Kujat, formerly the leader of the German armed forces and the chairman of the NATO Military Committee, outlined the deal: "Ukraine had pledged to renounce NATO membership and not to allow any foreign troops or military installations to be stationed," while "Russia had apparently agreed to withdraw its forces to the level of February 23, i.e. before the attack on Ukraine began." However, Kujat asserts that "British Prime Minister Boris Johnson intervened in Kiev on 9th April and prevented a signing. His reasoning was that the West was not ready for an end to the war" (Helmer 2023). According to Kujat, the West set conditions for negotiations that were equivalent to capitulation to ensure that the war would continue: "Now the complete withdrawal is repeatedly demanded as a prerequisite for negotiations" (Helmer 2023).

In June 2022, Boris Johnson argued in an address to the G7 and NATO that "now is not the time to settle and encourage the Ukrainians to settle for a bad peace" and instead he advocated "strategic endurance" (Webber 2022). In an op-ed, Boris Johnson (2022) rejected any negotiations: "The war in Ukraine can end only with Vladimir Putin's defeat."

The Atlantic Council later hosted Boris Johnson at an event where he argued that escalation should not be a concern: "How can we seriously worry about provoking [Putin] when we have seen what he will do without the slightest provocation?" Even the danger of nuclear war was casually dismissed by Johnson as Russia "won't use nuclear weapons," and even if a nuclear strike took place "the Ukrainians will probably fight on and win anyway" (Walla 2023).

Lloyd Austin, the U.S. Secretary of Defense and former board member of Raytheon, specifically outlined the objective of the war as to degrade Russia's military capabilities: "We want to see Russia weakened to the degree that it can't do the kinds of things that it has done in invading Ukraine" (Carbonaro 2022). U.S. Congressman Dan Crenshaw made his case for supplying weapons to Ukraine: "Investing in the destruction of our adversary's military, without losing a single American troop, strikes me as a good idea" (Lonas 2022). The Republican leader, Mitch McConnell (2022), was blunt in making the case for the pursuit of U.S. national interests: "President Zelenskyy is an inspiring leader. But the most basic reasons for continuing to help Ukraine degrade and defeat the Russian invaders are cold, hard, practical American interests." In a testimony, retired U.S. General Keith Kellogg argued that using Ukrainians rather than U.S. troops to defeat Russia as a strategic adversary is the "acme of professionalism." Republican Senator Lindsey Graham also opined the U.S. was in an ideal position as it could fight Russia to the last Ukrainian: "I like the structural path we're on here. As long as we help Ukraine with the weapons they need and the economic support, they will fight to the last person" (Maté 2022a). Chas Freeman, the former U.S. Assistant Secretary of Defense for International Security Affairs and Director for Chinese Affairs at the U.S. State Department, was unhappy with this U.S. policy and argued that unfortunately "we will fight to the last Ukrainian.... Everything we are doing, rather than accelerating an end to the fighting and some compromise, seems to be aimed at prolonging the fighting" (Maté 2022b).

The objective of defeating Russia has been eagerly promoted by the think tanks. Eliot Cohen from the Center for Strategic and

International Studies (CSIS), penned an article in *The Atlantic* with the title: "It's Not Enough for Ukraine to Win. Russia has to Lose." Cohen argues that "the West must not only aid in the defeat of Russia—it must convince Russia that it has been defeated," which would also send a powerful signal to Beijing (Cohen 2023). A defeat also means Ukraine's "speedy accession to the EU and NATO, but also a deep Western commitment to rebuilding Ukraine economically and, most important, arming it to the teeth for years to come." Furthermore, "the West needs an aggressive information campaign to drive home the reality of Russian defeat":

> Information warfare should be reinforced by continued sanctions, whose aim is not so much to win the war as to cripple Russian war-making potential for the long run by depressing the economy and forcing Russia to make do with inferior components and spare parts (Cohen (2023).

Benjamin Freeman, a research fellow at the Quincy Institute focusing on money in politics and think tanks, notes concerning the Cohen article that "every single one of the weapons the author recommends the U.S. give Ukraine are made by funders of the author's employer. . . . This should be disclosed in the article." Freeman thus criticizes the special interest of both Eliot Cohen and CSIS in pushing for increased confrontation, as well as the failure of *The Atlantic* to disclose that special interest.

While most of the think tanks maintain a hawkish approach to the war in Ukraine that favors continued escalation, there have been some notable exceptions. RAND, which outlined an extensive strategy in 2019 about using Ukraine to weaken Russia, published another report in January 2023 with the title "Avoiding a Long War." The report notes that despite the "optimism about Kyiv's prospects," there are grave risks that will increase over time (RAND 2023: 1). The report warns that the war could result in the possible use of nuclear weapons, or an escalation to a direct war between NATO and Russia. Furthermore, a long war will create growing economic pain for both Ukraine and Europe, and make it less likely that Ukrainian refugees will ever return. The U.S. funding of the war also will become an increasing economic burden and distracts from other foreign policy priorities such as China. With the rise in energy and food prices, the entire global economy will suffer, which also results in political instability. Last, Russia could gain more territories and also become more reliant on, and thus "subordinated" to, China (RAND 2013: 11).

Thoughtless Think Tanks Shape the Ukrainian War Discourse

Flush with funding from the booming business of the Military-Industrial Complex, the think tanks have great influence in shaping the discourse on the war in the media and among policymakers. The inherent biases and ideological orientations of the think tanks inescapably create one-sided perspectives and analyses. During the war in Ukraine, they have overwhelmingly been devoted to storytelling and selective framing with simplified portrayals of good versus evil. The absence of research into or discussions about negotiations and diplomacy reveals that the think tanks do not prioritize peaceful solutions, diplomatic initiatives, and reconciliation to build a common peace—or even consider them, rather they have become a key instrument of the war propaganda. They do not, in short, "think" about the issues.

The role of think tanks in generating and advancing the war propaganda has obstructed their ability to address both the actualities and the likely consequences of the war—and accordingly to provide wise counsel to policymakers. Addressing the reluctance of the vast majority of the world to send weapons to Ukraine and impose sanctions on Russia would conflict with the narrative of Russia being isolated by the "international community." But the West's unprecedented sanctions against Russia are not deemed to be legitimate by a large part of the world, who are therefore concerned about the West's exorbitant influence in the international economic system. Freezing and stealing the money of the Russian Central Bank is celebrated within the West as a display of virtue, while in much of the world it is an indication of the West abandoning the rule of law and some of the most basic principles of international trade and commerce.

Accordingly, the West's role in provoking and prolonging the war and its use of sanctions has intensified global efforts to reduce reliance on the West. Most countries outside NATO are eagerly deepening economic ties with Russia as huge market shares were opened due to the evacuation of Western companies due to the restrictions imposed by its sanctions. The former influence of the West in Russia, due to Russia's deep economic dependence on the West, has come to an end. On a wider scale, an international effort towards de-dollarization and a more general de-Americanization of industries has taken a major leap towards a "post-Western world." The West was not able to achieve decisive victory on the battlefield, was not able to destroy the Russian economy, and could not achieve international isolation of Russia.

Yet the West faces a limited ability to correct its failed policies. The Manichean narratives of good versus evil preserved in the echo chambers that think tanks continue to contribute to creating are by design difficult to challenge. As Lippman cautioned, war propaganda contributes greatly to mobilizing the masses against an adversary, yet it obstructs a workable peace.

21. Conclusion: Transparency Is Required to Restore the Purpose of Think Tanks

The book was intended as an introduction to the power and influence of the think tank racket over policies toward Russia. It is not meant to be encyclopedic or definitive. That can be left to someone with more time on their hands, and a broader view.

Think tanks have strayed far from their initial function of informing elected officials, and have now an immensely corrupting impact on politics due to the business model that think tanks follow. Think tanks can subvert democracy and obstruct a foreign policy aimed to maximize security, which is especially dangerous when dealing with policies towards a powerful state such as Russia.

The focus here has been Russia because the main financers of think tanks are weapons manufacturers, and conflict with Russia is big business for this industry. The financial incentives for continuing conflict with Russia after the Cold War, a common denominator for most think tanks, have had a disastrous influence on foreign policy. In the 1990s, the dominant foreign policy objective of Russia was merely to integrate with the West and overcome the Cold War dividing lines. 30 years later, NATO and Russia are fighting a proxy war in Ukraine and the political debates are all about a struggle between good and evil, with no constructive diplomacy in sight. This is not 1956 or 1968 when the Red Army marched into Budapest and Prague. The Soviet Union no longer exists, and communism is over. While the USSR had its own economic system, independent of the West, Russia does not.

It is fully integrated into the global capitalist order. Russians have mortgages, car loans, and businesses to run. The state no longer takes care of everything.

However, the think tank racket's sponsors need the idea of an aggressive and revanchist Russia to maintain profits or justify their continued existence. Of course, it could be argued Moscow played into their hands by reabsorbing Crimea in 2014 and invading Ukraine in 2022. But what you will not see from these pressure groups is detailed explanations of Russian security concerns or why the pan-European security order collapsed. Sadly, for all who desire peace and stability in Europe, that was not good for the bottom line of the various vested interests which bankroll the think tank racket.

As explained earlier, arms makers saw the expansion of the U.S.-controlled alliance as an opportunity to open new markets. The way to "sell" NATO expansionism was to paint the idea that Russia was a threat in eastern Europe. NATO itself funds think tanks because its messaging helps keep the alliance alive, by convincing the media, and policymakers, that it still has some sort of purpose. The U.S. State Department's main motivation appears to be to provide "jobs for the boys," given that so many former U.S. diplomats and government figures end up in the think tank racket after leaving the political fray. Meanwhile, other actors from oil-rich gulf dictatorships to Ukrainian oligarchs throw in money to obtain access to powerful people in Washington and other western capitals. Basically, the whole thing is a massive money racket, chasing ghosts to keep the cash spigot open.

The influence of think tanks is not limited to foreign policy and can be found everywhere. From economics to education to medicine. Often it is nefarious, but sometimes, to be fair, the movement can be a force for good. The problem is that they are not transparent. Finances are frequently very murky, and it is very common for backers to obfuscate their input and agendas, using various foundations or cut-outs.

The lack of transparency becomes a threat to an open society. Case in point, George Soros has money channeled through foundations such as "New America," the "Open Society Foundations," "Human Rights Watch," "Scientists for EU," and "Best for Britain." His operations have been pushed out of countries as disparate as Uganda, Russia, and

Pakistan and he has been publicly denounced by governments ranging from Israel to Poland and that of his native country, Hungary. But we also have to accept that Soros has done plenty of good. While today Viktor Orban vilifies him in Budapest, back in 1989 he was one of more than 3,200 Hungarian students who Soros sponsored to study abroad. Between 1991 and 1996, he spent $5 million providing free breakfasts for Hungarian elementary school children and he has frequently delivered aid to Hungary in times of crisis, for instance, when during the red sludge pollution scandal in the Danube in 2010.

It is the financial power of Soros rather than the quality of his ideas that has determined his influence. For example, Soros's thoughts about constructing a new security order after the Cold War entailed using NATO to advance U.S. hegemony. Toward this end, Soros envisioned NATO partnering with Eastern European states to obtain cannon fodder. Western societies would find it difficult to accept large casualties among their own soldiers, while eastern Europeans would be more prepared to sacrifice their sons and daughters: "... the combination of manpower from Eastern Europe with the technical capabilities of NATO would greatly enhance the military potential of the Partnership because it would reduce the risk of body bags for NATO countries, which is the main constraint on their willingness to act" (Soros 1993).

One is free to make this argument, which can be scrutinized in a democratic debate. The problem is that these ideas are not discussed in the open, instead they are promoted with powerful financing. The External Affairs Minister of India, Subrahmanyam Jaishankar, remarked in 2023 why Soros was dangerous (Sen 2023):

> "Soros is an old, rich opinionated person sitting in New York who still thinks that his views should determine how the entire world works. Now if I would only stop at old, rich and opinionated, I would put it away. But he is old, rich, opinionated and dangerous. Because what happens is when such people actually invest resources in shaping narratives. People like him think an election is good if the person they

> want to see, wins and if the election throws up a different outcome then they will say it is a flawed democracy and the beauty is that all this is done under the pretense of advocacy of open society."

Let us say you are at home watching BBC or CNN and Edward Lucas or Anne Applebaum are brought on to discuss Russia. They will be introduced as "columnists for the Times" or "writers for The Atlantic." But the BBC host will never explain that they also work for CEPA, a think tank funded by weapons manufacturers who profit from tensions with Russia. This is the way the think tank racket operates: It uses the sheen of academia to get its lobbyists front and center in the media. Meanwhile, producers and journalists play along and nobody suffers any repercussions.

It is the public who is being misled. This is appalling when you think about it because experts should be trustworthy. After all, while free speech is important, paid-for speech is a different story. Surely it is essential for democracy, and fairness, that people can judge why commentators might be saying something? Their funding sources should be clearly outlined. Otherwise, broadcasters, online, and print publications are being completely dishonest, promoting paid-for influence without declaring the vested interests behind the scenes.

It seems the time has come for media outlets to introduce a new code of ethics on the use of think tanks. In the interests of transparency, their employees should be forced to disclose the main funders of their organizations. British NHS surgeon Clive Peedell, in 2018, led a campaign to force Britain's state broadcaster to comply with rules like this. He suggested that "failure to publicly declare this (financial) information should disqualify the organization from appearing on a BBC platform."

In reality, this needs to be adopted, industry-wide. But the problem is there is little incentive. Think tanks are increasingly taking advantage of tight news budgets to influence the press agenda in favor of their sponsors. The only solution is public pressure. What you are holding is an attempt to start a debate. The hope is it succeeds in this goal.

References

Abella, A. 2009. *Soldiers of Reason: The RAND corporation and the rise of the American empire*. Boston: Houghton Mifflin Harcourt.

Abelson, D.E. 2006. *Capitol Idea: Think tanks and U.S. foreign policy*. Montreal: McGill-Queen's University Press.

———. 2014. "Old world, new world: the evolution and influence of foreign affairs think-tanks." *International Affairs* 90(1): 125–42.

AEI (American Enterprise Institute). 2001. "Think Tanks Look at Missile Defense." AEI, 4 March 2001.

Ahmed, N. 2014. "Think tank behind Tory foreign policy promotes Arab world fossil fuel hegemony." *The Guardian,* 7 May 2014.

Asmus, R.D. 2003. "Having an impact: Think Tanks and the NATO enlargement debate." *Connections* 2(1): 91–94.

Atlantic Council. 2014. Remarks by Vice President Joe Biden at the Atlantic Council's Toward a Europe Whole and Free Conference. Atlantic Council, 30 April 2014.

———. 2015. "Preserving Ukraine's Independence, Resisting Russian Aggression: What the United States and NATO Must Do." Atlantic Council, February 2015.

———. 2016. "Explainer: Five things about the Ukraine controversy you need to know (plus a freebie)." Atlantic Council, 26 September 2019.

———. 2019. "Why Poroshenko doesn't deserve a second term." Atlantic Council, 28 February 2019.

———. 2020. *Annual Report: Shaping the Global Future Together.* Atlantic Council, 2020.

Babst, S. 2010. "Public diplomacy and the NATO brand: The Alliance's ongoing battle for hearts and minds in an ever more clustered media environment." *Business Ukraine Online* 4(9): 1–2.

Baker, J. 2002. Russia in NATO? *The Washington Quarterly* 25(1): 95–103.

BBC. 2014a. Ukraine crisis: Transcript of leaked Nuland-Pyatt call. *BBC*, 7 February 2014.

———. 2014b. "Ukraine's revolution and the far right." *BBC*, 7 March 2014.

———. 2014c. "Ukrainian forces withdraw from Crimea." *BBC*, 24 March 2014.

———. 2016. "Kvartira Leshchenko's apartment: NABU nashlo priznaki korruptsii" ["NABU found signs of corruption"]. *BBC*, 19 September 2016.

———. 2018. "European security in a post-Nato world?" *BBC*, 5 July 2018.

———. 2019a. "Does taxing rich people more put the brakes on innovation?" *BBC*, 11 February 2019.

———. 2019b. "Ukraine election: Comedian Zelensky wins presidency by landslide." *BBC*, 22 April 2019.

———. 2020. "Coronavirus: Russia brings army doctors home from Italy." *BBC*, 6 May 2020.

BBG. 2014. "Media and News During the Crisis in Ukraine." *BBG*, June 2014.

Bennett, G. 2018. *The Zinoviev Letter: The Conspiracy that Never Dies*. Oxford: Oxford University Press.

Bernays, E. 1928. *Propaganda*. New York: Liveright.

Bidder, B. 2015. "Expert Criticizes Allegations of Russian MH17 Manipulation." *Spiegel International*, 4 June 2015.

Bjorgaas, T. 2012. NOREF Report: "From Contributor to Partner? Norway's role in foreign policy research and implementation in the United States." *NOREF*, May 2012.

Blank, S. 2016. "Putin's Next Potential Target: The Baltic States." Atlantic Council, 5 Januray 2016.

———. 2020. "U.S. Should Revive Lend-Lease to Contain Russia." Atlantic Council, 2 May 2020.

Blumenthal, M. 2018. "Inside the temple of covert propaganda: The Integrity Initiative and the UK's scandalous information war." *The Grayzone*, 17 December 2018.

Bogen, O. 2021. "Professor beskyldes for å drive russisk propaganda fra norsk universitet" ["Professor is accused of running Russian propaganda from a Norwegian university"]. *TV2,* 5 February 2021.

Borger, J. 2016. "Russian hostility 'partly caused by west,' claims former US defence head." *The Guardian*, 9 March 2016.

Braw, E. 2019. "Stop Worrying and Learn to Love the Military-Industrial Complex." *The Wall Street Journal*, 2 January 2019.

Browning, C.S. 2003. "The Region-Building Approach Revisited: The Continued Othering of Russia in Discourses of Region-Building in the European North." *Geopolitics* 8(1): 45–71.

Burch, S. 2018. "Larry King Slams Former Network CNN: 'Stopped Doing News a Long Time Ago.'" *The Wrap*, 8 November 2018.

Burns, W. 2008. "Nyet means nyet: Russia's NATO Enlargement Redlines." *Wikileaks*, 1 February 2008.

Bush, G. H. W. 1992. Address Before a Joint Session of the Congress on the State of the Union. *The American Presidency Project*, 28 January 1992.

Caldwell, C. 2022. "The War in Ukraine May Be Impossible to Stop. And the U.S. Deserves Much of the Blame." *The New York Times*, 31 May 2022.

CANE. 1998. "Founding Declaration of the Coalition Against NATO Expansion." CANE, 26 January 1998.

Capaccio, A. 2019. "BAE Nears U.S. Army Approval of $10 Billion Howitzer Project After Years of Flaws." *Bloomberg,* 15 October 2019.

Carbonaro, G. 2022. "U.S. Wants Russia 'Weakened' So It Can Never Invade Again." *Newsweek,* 25 April 2022.

Carden, J. 2016. "Congress Has Removed a Ban on Funding Neo-Nazis From Its Year-End Spending Bill." *The Nation*, 14 January 2016.

Carpenter, T. G., and B. Conry, eds. 1998. *NATO Enlargement: Illusions and Reality*. Cato Institute.

Carpenter, T. G. 2017. "America's Ukraine Hypocrisy." CATO Institute, 6 August 2017.

CEPA. 2017. "Winter is Coming." CEPA, 18 October 2017.

Chandrasekaran, R. 2012. "Civilian analysts gained Petraeus's ear while he was commander in Afghanistan." *The Washington Post,* 18 December 2012.

Chatham. 2019. "The Kremlin Spectrum: Western Approaches Towards Russia." Chatham House, 14 May 2019.

Clifton, A., and B. Freeman. 2021. "Can we make think tanks great again?" Responsible Statecraft, 12 May 2021.

Clifton, E. 2023. "Arms industry titan poised to sit on Council on Foreign Relations board." Responsible Statecraft, 18 May 2023.

Clinton, B. 1994. Remarks to Multinational Audience of Future Leaders of Europe. U.S. Diplomatic Mission to Germany, 9 January 1994.

Clover, C. 2012. "Clinton vows to thwart new Soviet Union." *Financial Times*, 7 December 2012.

Cohen, S. F. 2009. *Soviet Fates and Lost Alternatives: From Stalinism to the New Cold War*. New York: Columbia University Press.

Connelly, T. 2017. "British think tank funded by Japan pushing anti-China campaign into mainstream UK media." *The Drum*, 29 January 2017.

Cousins, N. 1987. *The Pathology of Power*. New York: Norton.

Crozier, M., S.P. Huntington, and J. Watanuki. 1975. *The Crisis of Democracy*. New York: New York University Press.

CSIS. 2019. "Syria in the Gray Zone." Center for Strategic and International Studies, 1 November 2019.

Cullison, A. 2019. "Ukraine Company's Campaign to Burnish Its Image Stretched Beyond Hunter Biden." *The Wall Street Journal*, 7 November 2019.

Czuperski, M., J. Herbst, E. Higgins, F. Hof, and B. Nimmo. 2016. "Distract, Deceive, Destroy: Putin at War in Syria." Atlantic Council, April 2016.

Daalder, I., and J. Lindsay. 2004. "An Alliance of Democracies." *The Washington Post*, 23 May 2004.

Daily Record. 2019. "Integrity Initiative outliers are the real 'useful idiots' in political Twitter storm." *Daily Record,* 7 April 2019.

De Tocqueville, A. 2003. *Democracy in America.* New York: Barnes & Noble Books.

Delauney, G. 2018. "Nato and Serbia put bombing behind them." *BBC*, 10 October 2018.

Dickinson, P. 2018. "Reluctant Russophobes: The Underwhelming International Response to Putin's Hybrid War." Atlantic Council, 4 March 2020.

Diesen, G. 2015. *EU and NATO Relations with Russia: After the Collapse of the Soviet Union*. London: Routledge.

———. 2022. *Russophobia: Propaganda in International Politics*. London: Palgrave Macmillan.

DPG (Defense Planning Guidance). 1992. *Defense Planning Guidance*. Washington, D.C.: U.S. Department of Defense, 18 February 1992.

Dutta, P. K., S. Granados, and M. Ovaska. 2022. "On the edge of war." *Reuters*, 26 January 2022.

Economist. 2019. "Can think-tanks survive a post-fact world?" *The Economist*, 29 May 2019.

Episkopos, M. 2021. "Was Brookings the Hidden Hand Behind the Steele Dossier?" The National Interest, 8 November 2021.

Euronews. 2022. "Ukraine war to be 'decided on the battlefield,' NATO official says." *Euronews*, 12 July 2022.

European Union. 2013. *EU-Ukraine Association Agreement* – the complete texts. European External Action Service.

Farkas, E. 2022. "The US Must Prepare for War Against Russia Over Ukraine." *Defense One*, 11 January 2022.

Findijs, A. 2022. "Democratic think tank plots war against Russia and China: What is the Center for a New American Security?" *World Socialist Web Site*, 16 November 2022.

Flint, H. 2012. "The Government, the Whistleblower and the Hollywood Starlet: Why a New Documentary Blames U.S. Department of Homeland Security for Brittany Murphy's Death." *Huffington Post,* 21 November 2012.

Flournoy, M. 2020. "How to Prevent a War in Asia The Erosion of American Deterrence Raises the Risk of Chinese Miscalculation." *Foreign Affairs*, 18 June 2020.

Forsyth, R. 2016. "Russia's Hybrid Warfare Is Harming Germany." Atlantic Council, 12 May 2016.

Foucault, M. 2019. *The History of Sexuality: The Will to Knowledge*. London: Penguin.

Frank, T. 2006. "Thus Spake Zinsmeister." *The New York Times*, 25 August 2006.

Freeman, B. 2020a. "Foreign Funding of Think Tanks in America." Foreign Influence Transparency Initiative, January 2020.

———. 2020b. "U.S. Government and Defense Contractor Funding of America's Top 50 Think Tanks." Foreign Influence Transparency Initiative, October 2020.

Friedman, T. L. 1998. "Foreign Affairs; Now a Word From X." *The New York Times*, 2 May 1998.

Friedman, G. 2014. "The interests of the Russian Federation and the United States in relation to Ukraine are incompatible with each other." *Kommersant*, 19 December 2014.

Gates, R. M. 2014. *Duty: Memoirs of a Secretary at War*. New York: Knopf Doubleday Publishing Grou.

Gerth, J., and T. Weiner. 1997. "Arms Makers See Bonanza In Selling NATO Expansion." *The New York Times*, 29 June 1997.

Gheciu, A. 2005. *NATO in the "New Europe": The politics of international socialization after the Cold War*. Stanford University Press.

Golovchenko, Y., M. Hartmann, and R. Adler-Nissen. 2018. "State, media and civil society in the information warfare over Ukraine: Citizen curators of digital disinformation." *International Affairs* 94(5): 975–94.

Goncharenko, O. 2020. "The Lesson of Crimea: Appeasement Never Works." Atlantic Council, 27 February 2020.

Greer, S., and M. Shtekel. 2020. "Ukraine's Navy: A Tale Of Betrayal, Loyalty, And Revival." *RFE/RL*, 27 April 2020.

Griffin, T., H. Aked, D. Miller, and S. Marusek. 2015. *The Henry Jackson Society and the degeneration of British neoconservatism: Liberal interventionism, Islamophobia and the 'War on Terror.'* Public Interest Investigations.

Grytsenko, O. 2019. "'I'm not a loser': Zelensky clashes with veterans over Donbas disengagement." *Kyiv Post*, 28 October 2019.

Guardian. 2013. John McCain tells Ukraine protesters: "We are here to support your just cause." *The Guardian*, 15 December 2013.

Healy, P. 2007. "New Center Has Lots of Clinton Ties." *The New York Times*, 27 June 2007.

Heffernan, B. 2012. "Our Navy's show of force off Rockall." *Independent*, 13 October 2012.

Heinrichs, R. 2019. "The U.S. Should Withdraw from the Treaty on Open Skies." *National Review*, 29 October 2019.

Heinz, G. 2021. "American primacy on the menu for big industry donors at CNAS." Responsible Statecraft, 22 February 2021.

Heinz, B., and E. Jung. 2021. "The Military-Industrial-Think Tank Complex: Conflicts of Interest at the Center for a New American Security." Revolving Door Project, February 2021.

Helmer, J. 2015. "The Think-Tank that blasts from the past – The case of case, cronies against self-sacrifice in Europe." John Helmer blog, 2 February 2015.

———. 2023. "Whr. Gen. Kujat: Ukraine War is Lost, Germany Now Faces an Angry Russia…Alone." *Veterans Today*, 25 January 2023.

Higgins, E. 2016. "New Generation of Digital Detectives Fight to Keep Russia Honest." Atlantic Council, 13 July 2016.

Hildrebrandt, T., and G. di Lorenzo. 2022. "Hatten Sie gedacht, ich komme mit Pferdeschwanz?" ["Did you think I was coming with a ponytail?"]. *Zeit*, 7 December 2022.

Hill, F., and A. Stent. 2022. "The World Putin Wants How Distortions About the Past Feed Delusions About the Future." *Foreign Affairs*, September/October 2022.

Hixson, W. L. 1998. *Parting the Curtain: Propaganda, Culture, and the Cold War, 1945–1961*. New York: St. Martin's Griffin.

Hope, C. 2018. "Half of the Russians in London are spies, claims new report." *The Telegraph*, 5 November 2018.

Hovland, C. I., and W. Weiss. 1951. "The influence of source credibility on communication effectiveness." *Public Opinion Quarterly* 15(4): 635–50.

ICAN. 2021. "Complicit: 2020 Global Nuclear Weapons Spending." *International Campaign to Abolish Nuclear Weapons*, June 2021.

Ignatius, D. 1991. "Innocence abroad: The new world of spyless coups." *The Washington Post*, 22 September 1991.

Ioffe, J. 2019. "Here's Why Ukraine Pops Up in So Many U.S. Scandals." *GQ*, 6 October 2019.

ISW. 2023. "Russian Offensive Campaign Assessment." *Institute of War*, 25 March 2023.

Sen, Amiti. 2023. "Old, Rich, Opinionated and Dangerous." *The Hindu BusinessLine,* 18 February 2023

Jankowicz, N. 2019. "Five myths about Ukraine: There's no civil war. Corruption is getting better. And it's not 'the Ukraine.'" *The Washington Post*, 26 September 2019.

Johnson, B. 2022. "For a Quicker End to the Russia War, Step Up Aid to Ukraine." *Wall Street Journal*, 9 December 2022.

Kagan, R., and W. Kristol. 2000. "A Look at . . . America's Role." *The Washington Post*, 19 March 2000.

Kaonga, G. 2022. "Video of Joe Biden Warning of Russian Hostility if NATO Expands Resurfaces." *Newsweek*, 8 March 2022.

Kaplan, F. 2004. "Truth Stranger Than 'Strangelove.'" *The New York Times*, 10 October 2004.

Kempthorne, J. 2022. "NYT, WSJ Look to Hawks for Ukraine Expertise." *FAIR*, 2 December 2022.

Kennan, G. F. 1948. "Comments on the General Trend of U.S. Foreign Policy." *Kennan Papers*, 20 August 1948.

———. 1997. "A Fateful Error." *The New York Times*, 5 February 1997.

Kerbaj, R. 2017. "Rifkind a stooge in secret PR war on China." *The Times*, 29 January 2017.

KIIS. 2021. "Socio-political moods of the population of Ukraine." *Kyiv International Institute of Sociology*, 19 October 2021.

Kirkpatrick, D. D. 2022. "John R. Allen Resigns as Brookings President After Qatar Revelations." *The New York Times*, 12 June 2022.

Korniienko, A. 2019. "Thousands rally in Kyiv against Zelensky's plan to end war with Russia." *Kyiv Post*, 6 October 2019.

Kortunov, A. 2019. "How to Stop NATO." *Russian International Affairs Council,* 3 December 2019.

Lasswell, H. D. 1927. "The theory of political propaganda." *The American Political Science Review*, *21*(3): 627–31.

———. 1995. "Propaganda." In *Propaganda,* edited by Robert Jackall, 13–25. New York: New York University Press.

Lavrov, S. 2007. Spiegel Interview with Russian Foreign Minister Sergey Lavrov: "Everyone Ought to Stop Demonizing Russia." *Der Spiegel*, 7 February 2007.

Lazarus, B. 2019. "Russian ambassador to London who made mocking remarks about Salisbury poisoning is ordered home after revelations he worked as a Soviet spy." *Daily Mail,* 4 May 2019.

Lippman, W. 1922. *Public Opinion*. San Diego: Harcourt, Brace & Co.

———. 1955. *The Public Philosophy.* Boston: Little, Brown & Co.

Lipton, E. 2013. "Think Tank Plays Down Role of Donors." *The New York Times,* 13 December 2013.

Lipton, E., and B. Williams. 2014. "Foreign Powers Buy Influence at Think Tanks." *New York Times*, 6 September 2014.

———. 2016. "How Think Tanks Amplify Corporate America's Influence." *New York Times*, 7 August 2016.

Lister, T. 2020. "The Nexus Between Right-Wing Extremists in the United States and Ukraine." *CTC (Combating Terrorism Center at West Point) Sentinel* 13(4): 30–41.

Lizza, R., R. Bade, T. Palmeri, and E. Daniels. 2021. "Politico Playbook: Double trouble for Biden." *Politico*, 21 September 2021.

Lloyd, R., and T.A. Postol. 2014. "Possible Implications of Faulty US Technical Intelligence in the Damascus Nerve Agent Attack of August 21, 2013." MIT Science, Technology, and Global Security Working Group, 14 January 2014.

Lonas, L. 2022. "Crenshaw, Greene clash on Twitter: 'Still going after that slot on Russia Today.'" *The Hill,* 11 May 2022.

Lrt. 2022. "Putin's plan includes Baltics, says former NATO chief." *Lrt*, 19 July 2022.

MacDonald, B. 2017. "'Useful idiots?' George Soros' Prague lobbyists direct their fire at RT guests." *RT*, 21 October 2017.

Mackinnon, A. 2020. "Bellingcat Can Say What U.S. Intelligence Can't." *Foreign Policy,* 17 December 2020.

Majumdar, D. 2018. "Russia, America and NATO: Where Are They Headed." *The National Interest*, 13 July 2018.

Manthorpe, R., and A. J. Martin. 2018. "Political tweets, 'infowars' and a Russia: How a fake news row went mainstream." *Sky News*, 11 December 2018.

Maté, A. 2019. "Ukrainegate impeachment saga worsens US-Russia Cold War." *The Grayzone*, 13 November 2019.

———. 2021. "Bellingcaught: Who is the mysterious author of Bellingcat's attacks on OPCW whistleblower?" *The Grayzone*, 24 March 2021.

———. 2022a. "US, UK sabotaged peace deal because they 'don't care about Ukraine': fmr. NATO adviser." *The Grayzone*, 27 September 2022.

———. 2022b. "US fighting Russia 'to the last Ukrainian': veteran US diplomat." *The Grayzone*, 24 March 2022.

Matlock, J. F. 2010. *Superpower Illusions: How Myths and False Ideologies Led America Astray – and How to Return to Reality*. New Haven, Connecticut: Yale University Press.

McConnell, M. 2022. "McConnell on Zelenskyy Visit: Helping Ukraine Directly Serves Core American Interests." Mitch McConnell official website, 21 December 2022.

McFaul, M. 2021. "The U.S. and Ukraine need to reboot their relationship. Here's how they can do it." *The Washington Post*, 23 August 2021.

Mcgrath, C. 2019. "Premier League – Win tickets What is Putin up to? Secret Russian sub exercise beneath icy waters north of Scotland." *Daily Express,* 24 November 2022.

Mead, G. H. 1934. *Mind, Self and Society*. Chicago: University of Chicago Press.

Mearsheimer, J. J. 2014. "Why the Ukraine crisis is the West's fault: the liberal delusions that provoked Putin." *Foreign Affairs* 93(5): 77–89.

Melanovski, J. 2021. "Ukrainian President Zelensky deepens alliance with far right." *World Socialist Web Site,* 30 April 2021.

Merriam, C. E. 1925. *New Aspects of Politics*. Chicago: University of Chicago Press.

Mills, C. W. 1956. *The Power Elite*. New York: Oxford University Press.

McCartney, J., and M.S. McCartney. 2015. *America's War Machine: Vested Interests, Endless Conflicts*. New York: Macmillan.

McCroskey, J.C. 1966. "Scales for the measurement of ethos." *Speech Monographs* 33(1): 67–72.

Miller, D. 2004. "Information Dominance: The Philosophy of Total Propaganda Control?" In *War, Media, and Propaganda: A Global*

Perspective, edited by Y.R. Kamalipour and N. Snow, 7–16. New York: Rowman & Littlefield.

MoA. 2018. "British Government Runs Secret Anti-Russian Smear Campaigns." Moon of Alabama, 24 November 2018.

Morris, E. J., and G. Fonrouge. 2020. "Smoking-gun email reveals how Hunter Biden introduced Ukrainian businessman to VP dad." *New York Post*, 14 October 2020.

Morrow, W. 2018. "U.S. intelligence think tank conducted 'false flag' operation impersonating Russian election interference." *World Socialist Web Site*, 31 December 2018.

Möller, F. 2003. "Capitalizing of Difference: A Security Community or/as a Western Project." *Security Dialogue* 34(3): 315–28.

Moscow Times. 2018. "Russia 6th Largest Economy in World GDP Rankings." *The Moscow Times*, 13 July 2018.

MSNBC. 2022. Transcript: The Rachel Maddow Show, 2/28/22 Guests: Hillary Clinton, Alexander Prokhoren. *MSNBC*, 1 March 2022.

NATO. 2010. *NATO 2020: Assured Security; Dynamic Engagement: Analysis and Recommendations of the Group of Experts on a New Strategic Concept for NATO.* 17 May 2010.

———. 2011. "'Post-Orange Ukraine': Internal dynamics and foreign policy priorities." *NATO Parliamentary Assembly*, October 2011.

Neef, C., and M. Schepp. 2007. Interview with Alexander Solzhenitsyn. *The New York Times*, 23 July 2007.

Neumann, I. B. 1999. *Uses of the Other: The "East" in European Identity Formation.* Manchester: Manchester University Press.

New York Times. 2016. "Atlantic Council and Corporate Donors." *The New York Times*, 7 August 2016.

Norman, G. 2022. "Top US military official relays 'worst thing' Russia did before invading Ukraine." *Fox News*, 4 May 2022.

Nuland, V. 2015. "'Testimony on Ukraine' at Senate Foreign Relations Committee." *US Department of State*, 8 October 2015.

OSCR (Scottish Charity Regulator). 2019. Inquiry Report made under Section 33 of the Charities and Trustee Investment (Scotland) Act 2005: The Institute of Statecraft, Scottish Charity Number SC040870." OSCR, 4 November 2019.

Packer, G. "Obama's Iraq Problem." *The New Yorker*, 30 June 2008.

Panetta, L. 2022. "U.S. Is in a Proxy War With Russia: Panetta." *Bloomberg*, 17 March 2022.

Parry, R. 2015a. "CIA's Hidden Hand in 'Democracy' Groups." *Consortium News*, 8 January 2015.

———. 2015b. "U.S. House Admits Nazi Role in Ukraine." *Consortium News*, 12 June 2015.

Pesenti, M. 2019. "Ukraine's cultural revival is a matter of national security." Atlantic Council. 19 January 2021.

Pew. 2014. "Despite Concerns about Governance, Ukrainians Want to Remain One Country: Many Leery of Russian Influence, as Putin Gets Boost at Home." Pew Research Center, 8 May 2014.

Piketty, T. 2014. *Capital in the Twenty-First Century.* Cambridge, Mass.: Harvard University Press.

Poliakova, A. 2017. "Trump's Budget Cuts Seen as Detrimental to U.S. Effort to Fight Russian Propaganda." Atlantic Council, 30 June 2017.

Polityuk, P., and A. Zverev. 2017. "Why Ukrainian forces gave up Crimea without a fight – and NATO is alert." *Reuters*, 24 July 2017.

Prouvost, T. 2022. "Hollande: 'There will only be a way out of the conflict when Russia fails on the ground.'" *The Kyiv Independent*, 28 December 2022.

Putin, V. 2012. "Russia in a Changing World: Stable Priorities and New Opportunities, Meeting with Russian ambassadors and permanent representatives in international organisations." President of Russia, 9 July 2012.

RAND. 2008. *Unfolding the Future of the Long War: Motivations, Prospects, and Implications for the U.S. Army.* Pittsburgh: RAND Corporation.

———. 2019a. "Extending Russia: Competing from Advantageous Ground." RAND Corporation, 24 April 2019.

———. 2019b. "Deterring Russian Aggression in the Baltic States Through Resilience and Resistance." RAND Corporation, 15 April 2019.

———. 2023. "Avoiding a Long War U.S. Policy and the Trajectory of the Russia-Ukraine Conflict." RAND Corporation, January 2023.

Rapoza, K. 2015. "One Year After Russia Annexed Crimea, Locals Prefer Moscow To Kiev." *Forbes*, 20 March 2015.

Reznikov, O. 2020. "To Stop Putin, the Western World Must Revisit the 1994 Budapest Memorandum." Atlantic Council, 31 May 2020.

RFE/RL (Radio Free Europe / Radio Liberty). 2021a. "Britain Says G7 To Consider Mechanism To Counter Russian Disinformation." *Radio Free Europe / Radio Liberty*, 3 May 2021.

———. 2021b. "Russia's Proposal To Redraw European Security 'Unacceptable,' U.S. Says." *Radio Free Europe / Ratio Liberty*, 18 December 2021.

Robinson, P. 2020. "New York Times Moscow correspondent wanted: Must believe all conspiracy theories about Russia, hate Putin & ignore facts." *RT*, 21 November 2020.

———. 2022. "The Disinformation Industry – A Cure Worse than the Disease?" Centre for International Policy Studies, 25 January 2022.

Rojansky, M., and J. Shapiro. 2021. "Why Everyone Hates Think Tanks." *Foreign Policy*, 28 May 2021.

Roland, A. 2021. *Delta of Power: The Military-industrial Complex.* Baltimore: Hopkins Press.

Romerstein, H. 2009. "'Counterpropaganda': We can't win without it." In *Strategic influence: Public diplomacy, counterpropaganda, and political warfare,* edited by J.M. Waller, 137–80. Washington: The Institute of World Politics Press.

RT. 2017. "Soros-backed 'rank amateurs' forge RT contributor's signature under anti-Russia declaration." *RT,* 11 November 2017.

———. 2018a. "Grammar mistakes mean you're a paid Kremlin troll, says Atlantic Council fellow." *RT*, 4 April 2018.

———. 2018b. "'I've seen the censorship': Syrian blogger tells RT how she was labeled a 'Russian bot.'" *RT*, 23 April 2018.

———. 2018c. "Bellingcat blogger slammed on Twitter for refusing to debate MIT professor on Syria claims." *RT*, 10 April 2018.

———. 2018d. "MIT professor accuses Bellingcat's Higgins of enabling war criminals to walk free in Syria." *RT*, 21 October 2018.

———. 2018e. "Atlantic Council: Pro-NATO pressure group uses distortions to fight 'disinformation.'" *RT*, 8 June 2018.

———. 2018f. "Former Ukrainian neo-Nazi leader speaks at NATO think tank event as it laments rise of right." *RT*, 2 July 2018.

———. 2020. "Coronavirus may be a product of US 'biological attack' aimed at Iran & China, IRGC chief claims." *RT,* 5 May 2020.

Rumsfeld, D. 2003. *U.S. Department of Defense Prepared Statement for the Senate Appropriations Defense Subcommittee: 2004 Defense Budget Request.* Washington, D.C.: U.S. Department of Defense, 14 May 2003.

Russel, B. 1932. *Education and the Social Order*. London: Routledge.

Russell-Sluchansky, C. 2014. "Hersh, Higgins and MIT Rocket Scientists Weigh in on Syria Sarin Gas Attack." *Mint Press*, 15 April 2014.

Ryan, Danielle. 2018. "Neutral and unbiased? Why 'think tanks' lobby for war in Syria." *RT,* 17 April 2018.

Satariano, A. 2020. "He Combs the Web for Russian Bots. That Makes Him a Target." *The New York Times*, 9 February, 2020.

Scarborough, R. 2018. "Christopher Steele: Hillary Clinton was preparing to challenge 2016 election results." *The Washington Times*, 12 December 2018.

Scarborough, R. 2020. "Hillary Clinton behind plan to tie Trump to Russia, CIA warned FBI's Comey, Strzok." *The Washington Times*, 7 October 2020.

Schrad, M. L. 2015. "Putin Has Asperger's? Don't Flatter Him." *Politico*, 6 February 2015.

Seelve, K. 1998. "Arms Contractors spend to promote an expanded NATO." *The New York Times*, 30 March 1998.

Semler, S. 2022. "The Think Tanks Advising Congress on Military Spending Take Money From the Arms Industry." *Jacobin*, 24 September 2022.

Semonsen, R. 2023. "Former Israeli PM: West Blocked Russo-Ukraine Peace Deal." *The European Conservative*, 7 February 2023.

Sipri. 2023. "World military expenditure reaches new record high as European spending surges." Stockholm International Peace Research Institute, 24 April 2023.

Small, M. 1998. "The Atlantic Council – The Early Years: Prepared for NATO as a report related to a Research Fellowship." NATO, 1 June 1998.

Spiegel. 2014. "The Right Wing's Role in Ukrainian Protests." *Spiegel*, 27 January 2014.

Spykman, N.J. 1942. *America's Strategy in World Politics: The United States and the Balance of Power*. New Brunswick: Transaction Publishers.

Snegovaya, M. 2014. "Ukraine's Crisis Is Not the West's Fault." *The Moscow Times*, 15 September 2014.

Sonne, P., and J. Grimaldi. 2014. "Biden's Son, Kerry Family Friend Join Ukrainian Gas Producer's Board." *The Wall Street Journal*, 13 May 2014.

Sood, V. 2020. *The Ultimate Goal: A Former R&AW Chief Deconstructs How Nations and Intelligence Agencies Construct Narratives*. New York: Harper Collins.

Soros, G. 1993. "Toward A New World Order: The Future of NATO." Open Society Foundations, 1 November 1993.

Staney, M. 2022. "If it's 'our war,' then we have a role to play in the peace." Responsible Statecraft, 16 May 2022.

Steele, J. 2004. "Ukraine's postmodern coup d'etat." *The Guardian*, 26 November 2004.

Stevenson, J. 2021. *A Drop of Treason*. Chicago: The University of Chicago Press.

Tass. 2020. "Russia sends 600 medical ventilators to Italy – ambassador." *Tass,* 25 May 2020.

Thompson, S., and D. Alba. 2022. "Fact and Mythmaking Blend in Ukraine's Information War." *The New York Times*, 8 March 2022.

Togoh, I. 2020. "From Russia With Love? Putin's Medical Supplies Gift To Coronavirus-Hit Italy Raises Questions." *Forbes*, 26 March 2020.

Traynor, I. 2004. "US campaign behind the turmoil in Kiev." *The Guardian*, 26 November 2004.

Trofimov, Y. 2020. "Viruspolitik at Play as Moscow Sends Soldiers to Help Italy." *The Wall Street Journal*, 31 March 2020.

Tyler, P. E. 1992. "US Strategy Plan Calls for Ensuring No Rivals Develop." *The New York Times*, 8 March 1992.

UK Parliament. 2018. "Foreign and Commonwealth Office: Integrity Initiative." UK Parliament, 27 November 2018.

U.S. Senate. 2011. "National Security and Foreign Policy Priorities in the Fiscal Year 2012: International Affairs Budget." Committee on Foreign Relations United States Senate, 2 March 2011.

Verseck, K. 2019. "Spiel's noch einmal, Wladimir." ["Play it again, Vladimir."] *Spiegel*, 17 January 2019.

Volker, K. 2022. "Buckle Up: This is Just the First Step." *CEPA*, 22 February 2022.

Vrabel, F., J. Janda, and V. Vichova. 2016. "How Russian Propaganda Portrays European Leaders." Atlantic Council, 16 August 2016.

Walla, K. 2023. "Boris Johnson: Stop worrying about Putin and 'focus entirely on Ukraine.'" Atlantic Council, 1 February 2023.

Webber, E. 2022. "Boris Johnson warns against seeking 'bad peace' in Ukraine." *Politico*, 23 June 2022.

Whelan, B. 2015. "How the far-right took top posts in Ukraine's power vacuum." *Channel 4*, 5 March 2014.

Wikileaks. 2007. "Norway: Missile Defence Public Diplomacy and Outreach." *Wikileaks*, 07OSLO248, 13 March 2007.

Williams, M.C., and I.B. Neumann. 2000. "From alliance to security community: NATO, Russia, and the power of identity." *Millennium* 29(2): 357–87.

Weaver, M. 2013. "How Brown Moses exposed Syrian arms trafficking from his front room." *The Guardian*, 21 March 2013.

White House. 2022. "Remarks by President Biden on Russia's Unprovoked and Unjustified Attack on Ukraine." The White House, 24 February 2022.

Williams, M. 2018. "EU vs Fake News: The truth about Brussels' fight against disinformation." *Channel 4 News*, 18 December 2018.

Zürn, M., and J.T. Checkel. 2005. "Getting socialized to build bridges: Constructivism and rationalism, Europe and the nation-state." *International Organization* 59(4): 1045–79.

Index

L

M

N